EVERYBODY'S
NATURAL FOODS COOKBOOK

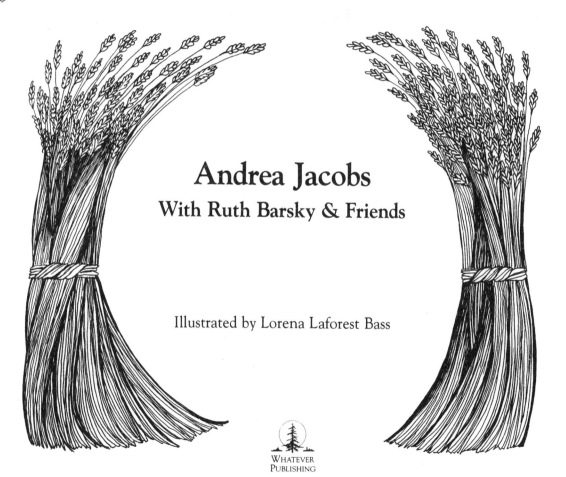

Andrea Jacobs

With Ruth Barsky & Friends

Illustrated by Lorena Laforest Bass

WHATEVER
PUBLISHING

Cover and text design by Lorena Laforest Bass
Production services by Michael Bass & Assoc.
Back cover photo by Richard Olsen

Published by Whatever Publishing, Inc.
P.O. Box 137
Mill Valley, CA 94941

First printing 1983

ISBN 0-931432-08-1

Distributed to the trade by:

Network, Inc.
P.O. Box 2246
Berkeley, CA 94702

This book is dedicated to everyone who wishes to enjoy a balanced, healthy, and natural way of eating and living.

A LITTLE HELP FROM MY FRIENDS

Sandra Althen
Mark Ballin
Denise
Letha Dolowitz
Barbara Edleson
Rona Foster
Sam Fins
Michael Gillotti
Maryanne Hall
Dennis Ichikawa
Judy Irvine
Diane Lander

Linda Mezay
Paul Nicholson
Pabini
Suzy Parker
Darryl Paul
Peter
Pat Rice
Sharon Scandur
Susan Stuart
Terri
Jan Whitby

SPECIAL THANKS

To Barbara Edleson for her inspiration and encouragement to do this book.

To Elizabeth Herron for the extra motivation to finish.

To Diane Lander for all her assistance and positive support.

To all my friends who contributed to this collection.

And an extra special thanks to Mark Allen and Lorena and Michael Bass for their fine production work.

CONTENTS

SOUPS & SANDWICHES

APPETIZERS & DIPS

BREADS & MUFFINS

THE MAIN COURSE & ACCESSORIES

DESSERTS & MUNCHIES

SMOOTHIES, ETC.

INTRODUCTION

Everybody's Natural Foods Cookbook is based on a flexible and relaxed way of cooking which involves creatively combining ingredients from your own cupboard and refrigerator, emphasizing improvisation and imagination. All the recipes are time-tested, healthy, and proven to be delicious as well as quick and easy to prepare. Numerous requests for my recipes led me to begin this book.

Cooking, whether for myself or for others, has always been a true love for me; to improvise a dinner from ingredients on hand has always been a challenge, never a problem. My background includes research with nutritionists and naturopathic doctors, cooking for "test recipe" parties, and experimentation with various diets (ranging from raw food to lacto-vegetarian), with occasional excursions into cooking with fish and chicken. Recent exploration into the catering and restaurant businesses has further broadened my culinary capacities.

The need for a different kind of cookbook became obvious when I investigated the vegetarian and natural foods cookbooks already on the market. These deal mainly with the substitution of eggs, cheese, and dairy products for meat, but place little emphasis upon creative, healthier combinations of foods, the use of simpler ingredients, and the exclusion of sugar. Many of the recipes in these books require exotic ingredients and long preparation times, offering little solace to novice vegetarians who wonder what else they can cook besides soybeans.

Everybody's Natural Foods Cookbook is for the beginner as well as the veteran vegetarian on the move, for those who don't want to spend all their waking hours in the kitchen, and for those who live alone and still want to be good to their taste buds and their bodies.

I believe that the cooking process can contribute to our total well-being. I encourage my readers to be inventive, take risks, trust the spirit of intuition, and have fun doing it. With a positive attitude we can all be creative cooks.

WE ARE ALL CREATIVE COOKS

The only magic involved in being a good cook is to love eating. If your taste buds respond to different flavors and textures, let them guide you to successful creations. If you selectively choose your ingredients, then taking a risk will rarely prove disastrous. Early experiments for yourself and a friend will build up confidence and show you how easy it is to be an inventive cook. I often make up recipes in the grocery store, where the vast selection of available foods is equivalent to the painter's palette.

Take a look down the aisle and think of dinner this evening. What appeals to you? Spaghetti? What texture and taste would combine well with spaghetti? Sour cream sounds good, perhaps with a little milk or cream to thin it out. Try it grated, sautéed with onion and butter. Add it to the sour cream mixture, pour generously over whole wheat spaghetti, and top it off with sunflower seeds. You've done it! A new recipe is born, and you're looking ahead to a delectable dinner.

Now what about the amounts of each ingredient? Experiment. Try a small amount and add to it until the texture is right. Then add seasonings. Don't worry about being exact; be creative and let your intuition be your guide. Have fun with it, keeping in mind the taste and texture and final appearance of the creation. Don't be afraid to use your imagination. Meals can be exciting to prepare and create, as well as healthy and delicious to eat.

Keep a folder of newly discovered recipes, recording amounts and proportions. Also, stock your cupboard with some of the basics suggested in the "Well-Stocked Cupboard and Kitchen" section. Let the recipes in this book serve as a guide and inspiration. The cupboard holds your paints; the kitchen is your easel and the table your canvas.

A WORD TO THE WISE...
(Or, How to Slip in a Few Soybeans)

Many of us live with very fussy and particular eaters. They may have had from 6 to 60 years to establish their eating habits and are usually resistant to change — especially to that strange stuff Mom has started to serve, or that organic something or other the kids are fixing for themselves. In working with families, I have often found the husband or teenager the most skeptical eaters. Introducing them to new and healthy foods requires a strategic approach.

A radical approach often backfires, and may lead to an outright refusal to try anything new. Therefore, it is wise to begin your substitutions slowly. Sometimes it is best to let them be surprised at how good something healthy can taste. Don't go into detail about what is in the particular dish and how good it is for them. Encourage taste first, questions later.

To begin this subtle transition, take some of the family's favorite meals and "clean 'em up." With spaghetti, for example, sauté mushrooms and onions, add fresh tomato sauce and your favorite vegetable (zucchini and broccoli are good) instead of meat. A little tahini adds protein and thickens the sauce; a few walnuts add protein and texture. Cook up some whole wheat pasta, smother with the sauce, sprinkle with fresh Parmesan cheese and voilà — a healthy, delicious, reasonably "normal" meal is yours.

Another good way to ease your family's transition from beef is to include more fish and poultry in your menu. Chicken can replace beef in many dishes, such as tacos and tostadas, with no loss of flavor. Ground turkey meat, available at many markets, makes great burgers and meat loaves. Some markets even carry turkey hot dogs. Don't throw out your old recipes. Good old macaroni and cheese never scares them off — only you know you have added fresh yogurt or kefir cheese to the raw cheddar and that the colored noodles are vegetable-based. The dish looks reasonably safe, tastes terrific, and initiates the taste buds to *real* foods.

Here are two of my favorite recipes that have brought compliments from little leaguers to grandpas:

Meal 1: Filet of Sole

Whole wheat dinner rolls
Green salad
Carrots in honey glacé
Filet of sole in white sauce
Grain or potato (optional)

Most supermarkets and health food stores carry common-looking dinner rolls made with whole grains. These taste delicious, especially when heated with butter. This substitution also begins the visual conversion from stark white to the earthy browns of healthier foods.

A green salad can be as simple as lettuce and tomato, or as complex as you like. Check your kitchen cupboards and experiment. In the beginning, most children like to have bacos or cheese chunks floating around; it gives them something to search for. Fresh toasted whole wheat croutons are great, as are sesame and sunflower seeds. Grated carrots or beets (if you can get away with them) add a nice dash of color. There are some excellent natural salad dressings on the market, or you can make up your own. (See Salads and Their Dressings.)

Carrots can be sliced fancy, steamed lightly, then coated with a heated mixture of butter, honey, a few squeezes of orange or lemon juice, and a touch of cinnamon.

Grease your baking pan with butter or line with foil. Lay fish filets across pan and cover with the following pre-mixed sauce: 1 carton Ricotta cheese, ½-1 t. garlic powder, VegeSal to taste, 2 T. white wine (optional), and the juice of 1 small lemon. Mix well and cover the fish, then grate Jack cheese over the top until fish is well covered. Sprinkle with parsley flakes and paprika. Bake at 375° until fish is tender but does not fall apart — about 20 minutes.

Meal 2: The Tofu Tostada

This is a full meal in itself.

Sauté in oil or butter one corn tortilla per serving. Be sure to pat off excess oil after cooking.

Line up on a tray, platter, or in bowls:

> Shredded lettuce
> Chopped tomatoes
> Chopped carrots
> Chopped scallions
> Grated cheese
> Homemade guacamole
> Sour cream or kefir cheese
> Hot sauce

Now mash up tofu (1 carton serves 4) into a buttered frying pan and sauté about 5-7 minutes, until warm. Add tamari or soy sauce (about ¼ c. per carton), and 1½ t. garlic powder. Cook over medium heat for 5 minutes.

Top tortilla with tofu mixture, then cover with grated cheese and a scoop of guacamole. Place on a cookie sheet in oven and cook until cheese melts, about 5 minutes. Remove from oven and cover with lettuce, tomatoes, carrots, scallions, hot sauce, and scoops of guacamole and sour cream. This is a true hit and a family favorite.

IDEAS FOR DESSERTS

Chocolate seems to be America's favorite sweet. If your family can't live without it (at least not yet!), use the same process of substitution outlined earlier. Revitalize your recipes with as many natural ingredients as possible. Buy high quality pure cocoa and unfiltered honey. Whole grain flours add quality and subtract preservatives.

Try our recipe for *Mandarin Chocolate Cheesecake* — it fooled the staff and patrons of a well-known French restaurant in Los Angeles. They had no idea there was no sugar in the cake and only ¾ cup of honey in the entire recipe. Watch your ingredients: pure cream cheese can be purchased at a health food store, along with graham crackers made with honey.

Carob looks like chocolate and is a good alternative, although the taste is an acquired one. Start slowly with carob chips or cookies instead of chocolate ones.

Delicious candies can be made from dried fruit, nut butters, and seeds.

The *Raw Banana Cream Pie* recipe in this book is fast, easy, and delicious, requiring neither sweeteners nor cooking time.

The blender can be a great dessert maker. Take that leftover Ricotta or cottage cheese, add a little milk, honey, and a flavoring (fruit, carob, preserves, cinnamon extract, etc.). Blend it up and serve in a custard dish, over strawberries, or tucked into a melon.

Desserts do not have to be saturated with sugar to taste or look good; nor do they have to be fattening. Be creative — nature has supplied us with a wide variety of naturally sweet foods to tempt and tantalize our palates.

THE QUICK, EASY WAY TO COOK GRAINS

Most grains can be cooked easily. The following recipe can be used for rice, millet, buckwheat groats, or bulgur wheat.

Put 2 cups of water in a saucepan and bring to a boil. Add 1 cup of grain and lower the flame to a simmer. Cover and cook until all the water has evaporated. Each grain has its own cooking time, so watch closely, but try not to open the lid too often. Brown rice usually takes from 35-45 minutes. The others vary, but usually require less time than brown rice.

Couscous is the easiest of all. Add 1 cup of couscous and 2 T. of Lemon herb or Italian salad dressing to 2 cups boiling water. Lower the flame, stir and simmer from 3-5 minutes. Do not quite cook all the water out of the pan. Cover, turn off the flame, and let stand for 8-10 minutes. Serve.

THE WELL-STOCKED CUPBOARD AND KITCHEN

Asterisks * indicate basic essentials. You do not need to stock the entire list; pick your favorites and experiment with the others.

Dry Goods

Almonds*
Baking Powder*
Baking Soda
Barley
Brown Rice*
Brown Sugar
Bulgur Wheat
Carob Chips
Carob Powder*
Cashews
Coconut

Couscous
Dates
Dried Fruit*
Dried Lima Beans
Dried Peas
Honey*
Lentils
Millet
Poppy Seeds
Powdered Skim Milk
Pumpkin Seeds
Raisins
Rye
Sesame Seeds*
Spinach Noodles
Sunflower Seeds*
Walnuts*
Wheat Germ
Whole Wheat Flour*
Whole Wheat Noodles
Whole Wheat Pastry Flour

Refrigerated and Dairy

Almond Butter
Apple Butter
Apple Cider Vinegar
Butter*
Chapatis
Cheese*
   Jack, Munster,
   Cheddar, Swiss,
   and Cream Cheese
Cottage Cheese*
Eggs*
Goat's Milk
Kefir
Lecithin
Miso*
Olive Oil
Raw Cream
Raw Milk*
Sesame Butter
Sesame Oil*
Sour Cream
Soy Sandwich Spread[1]
Tahini
Tofu*
Tortillas*
Wayfarers Bread
Yogurt*

[1]Many of these recipes call for soybean spread. You can use any packaged soybean spread, or any cooked, mashed beans, or bean dip.

Vegetables

Alfalfa Sprouts*
Asparagus
Avocados*
Bean Sprouts
Beets
Broccoli*
Cabbage
Cauliflower
Celery*
Cucumbers
Eggplant
Green Beans
Lettuce*
    Red, Romaine,
    Butter, Iceberg
Mushrooms*
Onions*
    Red, Yellow,
    Scallions
Parsley
Peas
Potatoes
Spinach*
Squash
Tomatoes*
Turnips
Yams
Zucchini*

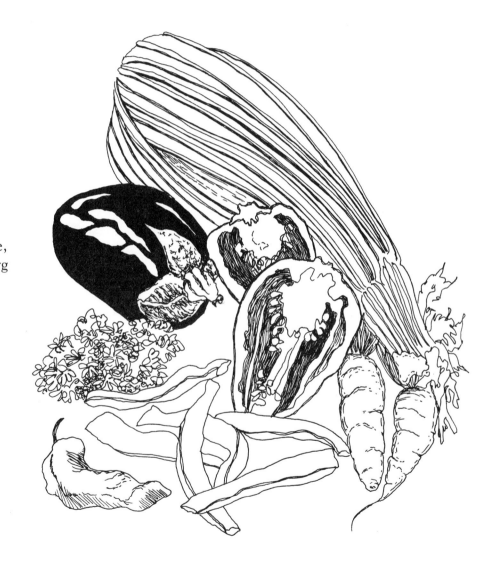

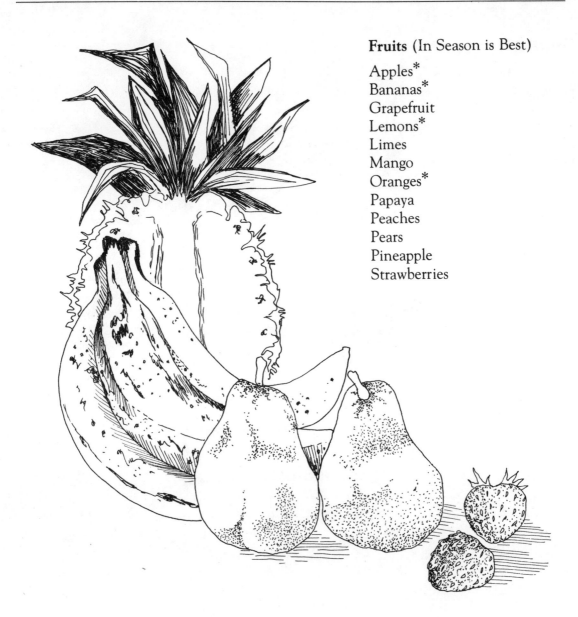

Fruits (In Season is Best)

Apples*
Bananas*
Grapefruit
Lemons*
Limes
Mango
Oranges*
Papaya
Peaches
Pears
Pineapple
Strawberries

Utensils & Necessities

Baking pans for breads,
   cakes, muffins,
   and brownies*
Blender*
Chopping Knife*
Cutting Board*
Fry Pan*
Grater*
Large soup kettle*
Mason or glass jars
Measuring cups and spoons
Refrigeration containers
Sauce pans*
Serving spoons
Soup ladle
Vegetable peeler and brush*
Wok
(A Food Processor
   is a real time saver.)

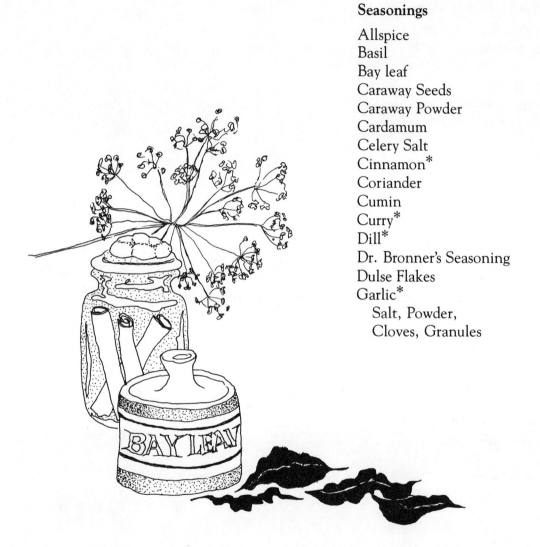

Seasonings

Allspice
Basil
Bay leaf
Caraway Seeds
Caraway Powder
Cardamum
Celery Salt
Cinnamon*
Coriander
Cumin
Curry*
Dill*
Dr. Bronner's Seasoning
Dulse Flakes
Garlic*
   Salt, Powder,
   Cloves, Granules

Ginger
Italian Seasoning*
Jensen's Seasoning*[2]
Mustard, dry and wet
Oregano
Protein Seasoning
Red and Black Pepper
Sea Salt*
Sesame Salt
Spike*
Tamari or Soy Sauce*
Tarragon
Thyme
Tumeric
Vanilla Extract*
VegeSal*

[2]Dr. Jensen's Vegetable Seasoning can be found in most
health food stores. It says "Bernard Jensen's Seasoning" on the jar. If unavailable any vegetable broth
powder or seasoning salt will do.

NOTES FOR BEGINNERS

These recipes which follow are only guidelines; experiment with amounts and seasonings to meet your own desires and tastes. Feel free to change the recipe whenever the spirit moves you! Innovate if you don't have all the ingredients.

Abbreviations used throughout: T. = tablespoon; t. = teaspoon; c. = cup; qt. = quart; pkg. = package.

Regardless of whether "sea salt" or just plain "salt" is called for, use either one. Sea salt is preferable. "Jensen's" is a seasoning with no salt; it can be interchanged with "VegeSal" or "Spike" (brand names available at your local store), although these two seasonings do have salt.

"Tamari" is an especially good brand name soy sauce. If you don't have it, use any kind of soy sauce, or "Dr. Bronner's Soya-Mineral Bouillon" (available at almost all health food stores).

Have fun with these recipes!

EATABLES

THE SALAD
& ITS
DRESSING

APPLE-CARROT-RAISIN SALAD

3 carrots, grated
1 apple, grated
½ c. raisins
¼ c. pineapple
¼ c. sunflower seeds
¼ c. sesame seeds
2 T. plain yogurt
½ c. coconut, grated

1. Mix all ingredients.
2. Add yogurt to moisten.

Serves 4-6.

BULGUR SALAD

1 c. uncooked bulgur
2 carrots, chopped
½ c. sprouts
½ c. sunflower seeds
½ mashed avocado
¼ t. apple cider vinegar
½ t. garlic powder or granules
Mayonnaise to desired consistency (about 2 T.)
Jensen's seasoning (or other)
Sea salt to taste

1. Cook bulgur in 2 c. water and cool.
2. Add the remaining ingredients to bulgur.

Serves about 4.

Good for quick summer lunches.

CAESAR'S SALAD

The Dressing:

1 clove garlic
⅓ c. olive oil
8 anchovy filets
1 T. Worchestershire sauce
½ t. salt
¼ t. salt
¼ t. Dijon-style mustard
1 t. capers with juice
⅓ c. sour cream
1 raw egg
Juice of 1 lemon

The Salad:

1 lb. shrimp
⅓ c. walnuts, chopped
1 large head romaine lettuce

1. Combine all dressing ingredients in blender at high speed.
2. Cut 2-4 slices of whole wheat bread into bite-sized pieces, and sprinkle with garlic powder. Toast until crisp.
3. Wash and dry well 1 large head romaine lettuce. Tear into bite-sized pieces.
4. Put lettuce in large bowl and cover with dressing.
5. Add croutons, 1 lb. shrimp, and ⅓ c. walnuts. Toss well.

Serves about 6.

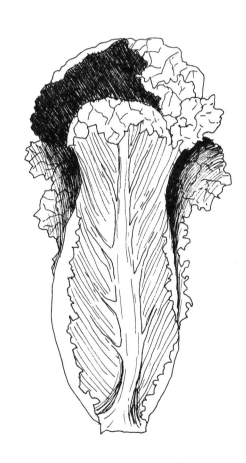

CARROT-CABBAGE SALAD

1 c. cabbage, shredded
1 c. carrot, grated
½ red onion, diced

1. Mix salad.
2. Serve with Cole Slaw Dressing.

Serves 4.

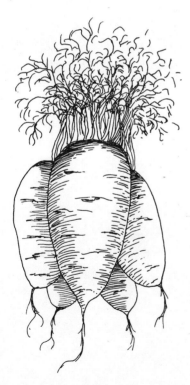

CHINESE CABBAGE SALAD

1 medium-sized chinese cabbage, sliced like cole slaw
2 c. bean sprouts
2 carrots, grated
2 celery stalks, chopped
¾ c. peas, shelled
½ c. flat green beans
½ c. sunflower seeds
¼ c. sesame seeds
1 small can water chestnuts
1 small can bamboo shoots

1. Mix all ingredients and chill.
2. Toss salad with Sweet Orange Dressing before serving.

Serves 6-8.

CURRIED CHICKEN SALAD IN PAPAYA (OR PINEAPPLE)

4 boneless chicken breasts
3 stalks celery, chopped
½ onion, chopped
¼-½ lb. mushrooms, diced
½ red pepper, chopped
¼-½ c. mayonnaise
1 T. tamari
¼ c. currants
½ t. garlic
½ c. sunflower seeds
1 T. orange juice
2 t. curry (or to taste)
2 papayas (or pineapples), halved
Sea salt to taste

1. Skin and chop chicken into cubes.
2. Sauté in butter until tender.
3. Add the remaining ingredients (except the papaya or pineapple) to the chicken cubes.
4. Mix and chill.
5. Serve in ½ papaya (or pineapple).

Serves 4.

Garnish with grapes and strawberries and sprinkle with coconut if you wish. Makes an attractive summer lunch.

CURRIED TUNA SALAD

1 large can of tuna, packed in water
2 stalks celery, diced
1 t. curry
½ t. VegeSal
Mayonnaise
Currants

1. Mix tuna and celery in a bowl.
2. Add enough mayonnaise to moisten well. Add VegeSal, curry, and a handful of currants. Mix well.
3. Chill and serve. Tastes great on a sandwich complemented with slices of avocado.

Serves 4.

An unusual alternative to the common tuna sandwich.

FOURTH OF JULY POTATO SALAD

14 large red potatoes
10 small eggs, hard boiled
2 avocados
1 small carton kefir cheese or sour cream
3 c. mayonnaise
1 red onion, chopped
1 bunch green onions, chopped
1 pkg. sprouts
1 c. sunflower seeds
5 stalks celery, diced
1 bunch spinach, cut up
1-2 T. apple cider vinegar
Juice of 1 lemon
Curry, garlic, Italian seasonings, VegeSal
    to taste

1. In large kettle, cut up and boil potatoes until cooked, but still firm.
2. Let potatoes cool, drain.
3. Combine all other ingredients in a bowl, except mayonnaise.
4. Add potatoes, then mayonnaise, and mix to desired consistency.

Serves a large party.

GARDEN GREEN SALAD

½ head romaine lettuce
1 tomato, chopped
¼ head cauliflower, chopped
½ c. carrots, grated
¼ c. apple, grated
½ cucumber, sliced
Sprouts
Sunflower seeds

1. Tear lettuce into bite-sized pieces, and add other ingredients.
2. Top with sunflower seeds and dressing.
3. Chill and serve.

Serves 4.

A fresh, crisp, and low-calorie salad.

Great with miso dressing.

GREEK SALAD AND OLIVE OIL DRESSING

The Salad:

2 cucumbers, peeled
6 medium tomatoes
1 green pepper
½ red onion
½ pt. Greek olives
¼ lb. feta or goat cheese

The Dressing:

5 T. olive oil
1 t. oregano, crumbled
Juice of ½ lemon
Sea salt to taste
Sprinkle of black pepper

1. Cut cucumbers and tomatoes into bite-sized pieces.
2. Slice green pepper and onion into thin slices.
3. Do not mix salad. Layer cucumber, tomato, green pepper, and onion. Cover with cheese and olives.
4. Mix dressing and pour over salad.

Serves 4-6.

HOT OR COLD RICE SALAD

1½ c. cooked brown rice
2 T. (heaping) mayonnaise
3-5 t. tamari
4 T. cottage cheese
½ box or bag sprouts
3 large green onions, chopped
½ avocado, mashed
¼ c. sunflower seeds
½ t. garlic
2 chopped carrots
Juice of ½ lemon
Herb salt

1. Combine all ingredients.
2. Serve hot or cold.

A low-cost, well-balanced salad. Good for potlucks.

LETHA'S EGGLESS EGG SALAD
(Tofu Salad)

1 lb. tofu
½ t. VegeSal
4 t. mustard (wet)
1 t. garlic granules
2 stalks celery, minced
3 green onions, minced
¼ c. sweet relish
1 T. soy sauce
½ c. mayonnaise (eggless)

1. Mix well with a fork.
2. Chill and serve.

Tastes great in a sandwich or on a bed of lettuce.

POTATO SALAD WITH MUSHROOMS

5 potatoes, unpeeled
2 c. fresh green beans, chopped in fourths
2 stalks celery, chopped
¼ lb. mushrooms, sliced
½ c. olives, chopped
2 hard-boiled eggs, chopped
½ c. Italian salad dressing
¼ c. white wine
1 T. tamari
½ c. mayonnaise
Dill
Salt and pepper to taste

1. Steam potatoes until tender.
2. Add Italian dressing to hot potatoes, and set aside.
3. Simmer green beans, celery, mushrooms, and olives in wine until tender, then add tamari.
4. Chop potatoes and add spices.
5. Combine with vegetables, then add egg and mayonnaise.
6. Chill at least two hours.

Serves 4-6.

RAW GRATED SALAD

On a bed of lettuce on a large plate, place:
A handful of grated carrots
A handful of grated beets
A handful of alfalfa sprouts
Diced avocado
Sunflower seeds
Sliced tomato

Cover with favorite dressing.

Makes a great diet plate, very colorful and delicious.

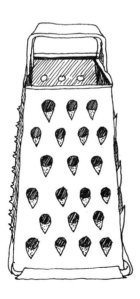

RAW POTATO SALAD

2 white potatoes, peeled
1 avocado
½ c. raw sunflower seeds
¼ c. parsley, chopped
½ c. sesame oil
1½ t. Jensen's or VegeSal
Juice of ½-1 lemon

1. Grate potatoes and cover with lemon juice.
2. Mix oil and seasoning together.
3. Chop parsley and avocado and add to potatoes.
4. Pour oil mixture over potatoes and top with sunflower seeds.

Serves 4.

Raw potatoes aid in digestion and can taste very good.

SPAGHETTI SALAD

1 head romaine lettuce, chopped
½ bunch scallions, chopped
½ lb. mushrooms, chopped
2 tomatoes, sliced
1 zucchini, diced
½ red onion, diced
½-¾ c. olive oil
Juice of 1 lemon
Garlic seasoning, to taste
Italian seasoning, to taste
Wine vinegar, to taste
Whole wheat spaghetti or pasta for 4 servings.

1. Cook whole wheat spaghetti, as directed on package.
2. Prepare salad.
3. Mix dressing.
4. Drain spaghetti in colander and rinse.
5. Pour spaghetti into salad and cover with dressing.
6. Serve and enjoy.

Serves 4-6.

A new and different experiment in salads.

SPINACH SALAD WITH PAPAYA

2 medium heads fresh spinach
1 bunch scallions
¾ lbs. mushrooms, sliced
1 whole fresh papaya, or 2 small cans mandarin oranges
1 avocado, diced
1½ c. croutons
Handful of sprouts
Sprinkle of toasted sesame seeds

1. Wash and dry spinach, remove stems and tear into bite-sized pieces.
2. Chop scallions finely.
3. Slice mushrooms.
4. Cube avocado and papaya.
5. Mix together all ingredients and top with sprouts and sesame seeds.
6. Chill and serve with your choice of dressing.

Serves 4-6.

A special and colorful salad.

SPROUT SALADS

Salads made predominately from sprouts are alive, full of vitamins A and C, and a good source of protein. Mix together any variety of sprouts — alfalfa, lentil, mung, wheat, pinto bean, and any others available. Add nuts, seeds, and sliced vegetables, and cover with dressing. Excellent for a light summer meal.

Try these salads with the special sprout dressings in the following section.

SWEET RAW POTATO SALAD

2 white potatoes, peeled
3 tomatoes, slightly boiled then peeled
2 T. sesame butter
½ t. cinnamon
½ c. oil (safflower or sesame)

1. Grate potatoes or put through food processor.
2. Mix all other ingredients and pour over potatoes.
3. Serve immediately.

Serves 2-3.

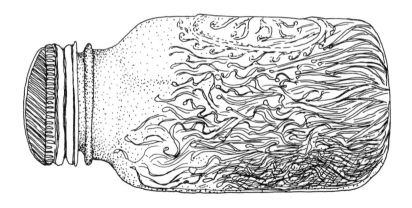

WINTER FRUIT SALAD & DRESSING

The Salad:

1 large red apple, chopped
1 medium yellow apple, chopped
2 bananas, sliced
2 tangerines
1 grapefruit
Any canned fruit, such as peaches or pears
    (homemade is best)
Pomegranate seeds, sprinkled in and used
    for topping

The Dressing:

6 T. white wine (optional)
2 T. honey
½ t. salt
1 small carton yogurt or whipped cream
Juice of 1 lemon

1. Slice all fruits (except pomegranate seeds), and put in bowl.
2. Mix together all dressing ingredients.
3. Add dressing to salad; top with pomegranate seeds.
4. Chill and serve.

Serves 4-6.

A luscious way to sweeten up your winter.

BASIC SALAD DRESSING

The basic ingredients for salad dressing are:
⅔ c. oil (sesame, corn, olive, soy, or safflower)
Juice of ½-1 lemon
Jensen's seasoning, VegeSal, or Spike

To the three ingredients above, try adding one or more of the following ingredients:
Avocado
Cooked soybeans
Sour cream
Cooked vegetables (spinach, zucchini)
Tomatoes, skinned
Cottage cheese
Nut butters and honey

Blend at medium speed.

Try different combinations and make up your own. Yogurt makes a good dressing for salads and fruits. Different seasonings such as dill, tamari, and cayenne pepper add different variations. Try curry or soy sauce with mayonnaise. Orange juice instead of lemon adds sweetness.

BUTTERMILK SALAD DRESSING

2 oz. buttermilk
½-⅔ c. oil (soy, sesame, or safflower)
½ t. sea salt
Juice of ½ lemon
Sprinkle of cayenne to taste

Blend in blender.

Serves 2-3 individual size salads.

Great over spinach.

CARAWAY SALAD DRESSING

¾ c. olive (or other) oil
¼ t. caraway
1 t. caraway seeds
¼ t. dry mustard
1 t. water
2 T. wine vinegar
Juice of 1 lemon
Garlic to taste

1. Place all ingredients except caraway seeds in blender.
2. Blend at medium speed.
3. Stir in caraway seeds and serve.

CITRUS-DILL DRESSING

½ c. sesame oil
1 t. lemon juice
2 T. orange juice
¼ t. curry
2 T. water
¼ t. sea salt
¼ t. coriander
1 t. apple cider vinegar
½ t. garlic salt
½ t. onion flakes
½ t. Jensen's seasoning
¼ t. honey
½ t. tamari
¾ t. dill
⅛ t. mustard
¼ t. cumin
⅛ t. ginger

Blend at medium speed.

COLE SLAW STYLE DRESSING

2 T. olive oil
2 T. sesame oil
1 egg yolk
3 t. apple cider vinegar
½ t. soy sauce
2 T. yogurt
Juice of ½ lemon
Vegetable salt (such as VegeSal)

Blend all ingredients at medium speed.

SOUR CREAM-GREEN GOURMET SALAD DRESSING

8 oz. sour cream
¾ c. sesame oil
½ c. cooked fresh spinach
3 T. Jensen's seasoning, or VegeSal, or Spike
½-¾ c. milk or half & half
Juice of 1 lemon
Garlic salt to taste

1. Mix all ingredients and blend at medium speed.
2. Chill.

Rich and impressive.

SPROUT SALAD DRESSING (SPICY)

⅓ c. sesame oil
⅛ c. water
2 T. lemon juice
⅛ t. thyme
⅛ t. basil
¼ t. mustard
¼ t. garlic powder
½ t. (just under) ginger
¼ t. honey
¼ t. tamari
½ t. sea salt

Blend at medium speed.

SPROUT SALAD DRESSING (TANGY)

⅓ c. sesame oil
⅛ c. water
3 T. lemon juice
⅛ t. pepper
¾ t. garlic
¾ t. onion flakes
½ t. sea salt
½ t. honey
1 t. apple cider vinegar
¼ t. mustard
⅛ t. parsley flakes

Blend at medium speed.

SPROUT SALAD DRESSING (ZESTY)

¼ t. ginger
½ c. sesame oil
4 t. lemon juice
1 t. Parmesan cheese
3½ T. water
½ t. garlic powder
½ t. onion flakes
½ t. Jensen's seasoning
½ t. sea salt
⅛ t. pepper
⅛ t. cumin
½ t. apple cider vinegar
¾ t. honey

Blend at medium speed.

SUZY'S ALL-PURPOSE MISO DRESSING

3 T. white miso (available in most health food stores)
¾ c. safflower oil
1 T. tamari
½ t. garlic granules
½ c. water
1 T. apple cider vinegar
1 green onion (top only), minced
1½ t. honey

1. Put all ingredients in blender.
2. Blend at medium speed until creamy, but not watery.

Serves about 4. Great with salads, over grains or as a sauce for fish.

SWEET ORANGE DRESSING

½-¾ c. sesame oil
½ t. Jensen's seasoning
½ t. honey
½ t. soy sauce
1 t. lemon juice
Juice of 1 small orange
Pinch of dry mustard

1. Place all ingredients in blender.
2. Blend at medium speed and serve.

Good over cabbage.

TOMATO TAHINI DRESSING

½ c. sesame oil
¼ t. sea salt
⅓ c. tomato juice
4 t. tahini
2 t. tamari
1 t. apple cider vinegar
½ t. garlic powder
⅛ t. curry
1 T. water
1 T. lemon juice
½ t. Jensen's seasoning
½ t. Italian seasoning
½ t. (heaping) honey

Blend at medium speed.

*A very different experience in salad dressing —
kind of spicy and creamy.*

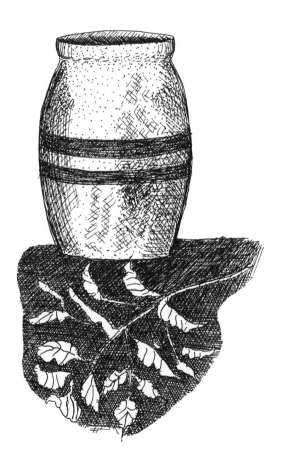

YOGURT-DILL SALAD DRESSING

½-⅔ c. sesame oil
½ c. plain yogurt
2 t. dill
2 T. mayonnaise
Juice of ½ lemon
Sea salt

1. Place all ingredients in blender.
2. Blend at medium speed, and serve.

YOGURT-MINT SALAD DRESSING

⅔ c. oil
½ c. plain yogurt
¼ t. honey
½ t. salt
Fresh mint to taste
Juice of ½-1 lime

Blend at medium speed and serve.

Good over fruit or green salad.

SOUPS AND SANDWICHES

AVOCADO SUPREME

Mayonnaise
Avocado, sliced
Mushrooms, sliced
Sour cream or cheese, or both
Sunflower seeds
Tomato, sliced
Baco-Bits
Sprouts or lettuce

Pile the ingredients between two pieces of your favorite bread.

Tastes great on toasted bread.

BROCCOLI CHEESE SOUP

1 small yellow onion, diced
1½ qts. water
1 large bunch broccoli, chopped
1 lb. sharp and smoked Cheddar cheese, grated
¾ c. milk
4-6 oz. sour cream
2 T. tamari
2 T. Jensen's seasoning or VegeSal
1 t. dill
Garlic powder
Sea salt to taste
Paprika

1. Simmer broccoli, onion, and seasonings until cooked, yet crunchy.
2. Add milk, sour cream, and grated cheese, tamari, salt, dill and garlic.

3. Stir until cheese melts.
4. Top with more grated cheese and paprika, and serve.

Serves 4-6.

This soup is a good crowd-pleaser.

CREAM OF SPINACH OR CHARD SOUP

1 bunch of spinach or chard, chopped
1 c. half & half
1 large carton sour cream
3 T. tamari
2 t. garlic powder or granules
2 qts. water
3 T. Vegetable Broth Powder
Sea salt to taste.

1. In a blender, food processor, or Vita Mix put half & half, sour cream, spinach (or chard), tamari and garlic. Mix on high until creamy.
2. In a soup pot put water and Vegetable Broth Powder. Heat until boiling, then lower to simmer.
3. Pour creamed spinach mixture into pot. Simmer about 30-45 minutes until cooked.

Serves 6-8.

A quick, easy cream soup.

CURRY PEA SOUP

1 c. split peas
1 c. celery, chopped
2 T. safflower oil
1 large potato, chopped fine
1 t. sea salt
2 bay leaves
1 t. garlic powder or granules
½ t. cumin
2 carrots, chopped
2 t. vegetable bouillon
4 t. curry (or to taste)
Yogurt, plain

1. In 1½ qts. of water, add vegetable bouillon, split peas, carrots, celery, oil, and potato. Simmer 1 hour.
2. Add salt, bay leaves, garlic, curry, and cumin. Simmer another 15 minutes.
3. Serve hot, topped with plain yogurt.

Serves about 6.

A hearty soup for a winter meal.

GAZPACHO
(Cold Spanish-Style Soup)

Serves approximately 4.

*Drop tomatoes in boiling water for 20-30 seconds; skin peels right off.

3 tomatoes, skinned* and chopped
1 green pepper, chopped
1 yellow onion, chopped
½ cucumber
3 sprigs parsley, chopped
½ c. olive oil
1 clove garlic, chopped
1 large zucchini, chopped
½ c. lemon juice
2 T. basil
Sprinkle of cayenne
Sea salt to taste
Bottled water, if needed
Hot sauce if desired

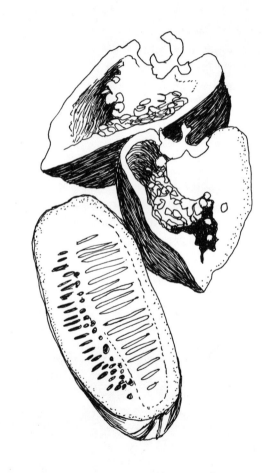

1. In a blender or food processor, add chopped zucchini, tomatoes, parsley, onion, garlic, green pepper, and cucumber.
2. Add lemon juice and olive oil. If necessary, prepare half the mixture at a time to avoid overloading blender or processor.
3. Combine all ingredients and serve cold with a celery stalk for decoration. Tastes great with tortilla chips.

GRILLED TOFU & CHEESE SANDWICH

2 cakes of tofu
½ c. cheese, grated
1 tomato, sliced
1 t. tamari
bread
butter

1. Grill bread on one side in buttered pan or on grill.
2. Mix tofu with tamari and place on one slice, then cover with grated cheese and tomato.
3. Place other slice on top and continue grilling, flipping sandwich from side to side until cheese melts.

Good with soup. Another variation is to add sliced mushrooms.

HEARTY ONION SOUP

1½-2 qts. water
5 T. Dr. Bronner's "All-1" seasoning (or tamari)
1 c. white onion, sliced
1 c. yellow onion, sliced
1 c. leek, sliced
¼ c. butter
1½ t. salt
1 T. honey
2 T. whole wheat flour
¼ c. dry sherry (optional)
1 t. Worchestershire sauce
4 slices French bread, toasted
½ c. Parmesan cheese, grated
1 c. Gruyere cheese, grated

1. Combine Dr. Bronner's seasoning and water and set aside.
2. Sauté onion in butter until brown. Add salt, flour, and honey. Stir until blended well.
3. Add broth, sherry, and Worchestershire sauce. Cover and cook at low heat for 30 minutes.
4. When serving, place one slice toasted bread in bowl, cover with soup, sprinkle Parmesan and Gruyere cheeses on top and broil until brown.

Serves 6.

LENTIL BARLEY STEW-SOUP

¼ c. (or less) soy butter
⅓ c. onions, chopped
3 stalks celery, chopped
2½ c. stewed tomatoes
2 c. water
½ c. dried lentils, picked over and washed
⅓ c. whole barley
½ t. sea salt
⅛ t. black pepper
⅛ t. thyme or rosemary
⅓ c. carrots, shredded

1. Melt soy butter in large heavy saucepan. Sauté onions until tender, add celery, and cook 5 minutes longer.
2. Add remaining ingredients except the carrots and bring to boil. Cover and simmer gently for 25 minutes, stirring occasionally.
3. Add carrots and cook 5 minutes longer, or until barley and lentils are tender.

Serves 4.

Hearty.

LENTIL SOUP

2 c. lentils
2 qts. water
¼ c. onion
½ t. garlic
2 bay leaves
2 c. tomatoes, diced
2 c. carrots, sliced
2 c. cabbage, shredded
2 c. zucchini, sliced
¼ c. soy sauce
1½ t. salt
2 t. basil

1. Combine lentils and water; bring to a boil and reduce heat.
2. Simmer 2 minutes before adding onion, garlic, bay leaves, tomatoes, and carrots.
3. Then add cabbage, zucchini, soy sauce, salt, pepper, and basil.
4. Cover and simmer until lentils are tender (about 1 hour).

Serves approximately 6.

PINK POTATO SOUP

1 onion, sliced
3 mixed-sized beets
3 small potatoes
3 carrots
2 zucchini
¼ lb. mushrooms
3 stalks celery
2 bay leaves
3 T. Jensen's seasoning
2 t. sea salt (or VegeSal)

1. Fill a large soup kettle with bottled water (3-4 qts). Start medium flame under kettle.
2. Cut onion in quarters and beets into chunks. Drop into water and simmer for 30 minutes. Water will be a deep red.
3. Add bite-sized pieces of carrots and potatoes, cover and cook another 20 minutes.
4. Add all seasonings at the end of the 20 minutes, together with the squash and mushrooms. Cover and cook for approximately 10-15 additional minutes. Check texture of vegetables to see they are still crunchy and not too soft or hard; cook accordingly. Tamari adds great taste.

Serves 6-8.

Can be kept overnight and served deliciously the next day.

SUZY'S CABBAGE-KASHA SOUP

1 medium-sized cabbage, shredded
2 onions, chopped
1 carrot, finely sliced
2 T. oil
2 T. whole wheat flour
5 c. water
½ c. buckwheat groats, toasted (kasha)
4 T. tamari
sea salt to taste

1. In soup pot, sauté onions, cabbage, and carrots, in that order.
2. Add water and bring to a boil.
3. Add buckwheat groats, flour (diluted in ⅓ c. water), sea salt, and tamari. Simmer 1 hour.

Serves 4.

THAI VEGETABLE SOUP

Serves 4-6.

Low in calories, high in protein.

2 qts. water
4. vegetable bouillon cubes
½ lb. mushrooms, chopped
2 stalks celery, sliced
1 large onion, sliced
1 bunch boy chok (or chinese cabbage), chopped
½ lb. bean sprouts
4 T. (heaping) peanut butter
¼ c. tamari
½ t. garlic granules
¼ t. cumin
1 t. curry
¼ t. cayenne pepper
2 cakes firm tofu, chopped into bite-sized pieces
Sea salt to taste

1. Bring water and bouillon cubes (or stock) to a boil in large soup pot.
2. Add chopped vegetables, lower flame and simmer until vegetables are slightly tender.
3. Add peanut butter, tofu cubes, and all seasonings. Stir well and let simmer another 5-10 minutes.

TOFUNA SANDWICH

1 cake tofu
1 small can tuna, packed in water, drained
½ red onion, chopped
½ c. sprouts
3 T. mayonnaise
½ t. garlic powder
Sea salt
Squeeze of lemon
Sweet pickle relish (optional)

1. Combine all ingredients in a bowl.
2. Make a sandwich with whole wheat bread, lettuce, and tomato.
3. Add Tofuna Spread and enjoy.

Makes about 4-6 sandwiches.

VEGETABLE STEW-SOUP

3 red potatoes, chopped
2 carrots, chopped
1 yellow onion, diced
1½ c. cooked couscous (Moroccan grain)*
3 T. miso
3 t. tamari
6-8 artichoke hearts (frozen is fine)
2 T. sour cream
Sea salt to taste

1. Fill large soup pan half-full with water and add chopped potatoes, carrots, and onion. Add miso and tamari.
2. Cook couscous as directed.
3. Thaw artichoke hearts and add to soup mixture together with cooked couscous.
4. Simmer until potatoes loosen, and stir in sour cream. Serve.

Serves 6-9.

Can usually be found in the gourmet section of your supermarket.

VEGGIE BURGER

There are many dry mixtures on the market for veggie burgers. Fantastic Foods puts out a good grain, seed, and vegetable mixture. Follow the instructions (usually just to add boiling water and let sit), then add grated carrots, chopped green onion, ground walnuts, and tamari. Grill or barbeque and put into a whole wheat bun smothered in the works — mayonnaise, mustard, ketchup, relish, tomato, and lettuce, and top with cheese.

APPETIZERS AND DIPS

ARTICHOKE SQUARES

2 jars marinated artichoke hearts
1 onion, chopped
1 clove garlic, diced
4 eggs
¼ t. hot sauce
¼ c. cracker crumbs
⅛ t. oregano
⅛ t. salt
⅛ t. pepper
½ lb. cheddar cheese, grated

1. Preheat oven to 325°.
2. Drain 1 jar of artichoke hearts into a bowl.
3. Take the other jar and pour into a fry pan with onion and garlic.
4. Sauté until browned.
5. Mix together remaining ingredients except cheese and add to bowl of artichoke hearts.
6. Pour fry pan mixture in.
7. Add ½ lb. grated Cheddar cheese and place into a rectangular baking pan.
8. Bake at 325° for 30 minutes, or until mixture sets.
9. Remove from oven, cool, and cut into squares.

Serves 6 plus.

Serve warm or cold. Great as an appetizer or side dish.

BROILED TOFU APPETIZER

1 pkg. tofu
Tamari
Garlic powder

1. Pre-heat oven to broil.
2. Slice tofu cakes into wafer-thin strips about 2″-by-¾″.
3. Soak them in a mixture of tamari and garlic powder.
4. Place them in a shallow pan (lined with foil) and pour remaining liquid over them.
5. Broil in oven (turning once to get both sides) about 15 minutes.

Serve warm or cold. A great-tasting mystery food.

BROWN RICE BALLS

1 c. rice cooked in 2 c. water
1 carton Ricotta cheese
½ t. garlic powder
1½-2 t. Jensen's seasoning
Toasted sesame seeds

1. Cook and slightly cool rice.
2. Add blended seasoning and Ricotta cheese.
3. Shape into bite-sized balls.
4. Roll in dish of sesame seeds.

Serve as an appetizer.

DENNY'S TAMARI DIP

½ c. mayonnaise
2 T. tamari, or to taste

Tastes great with vegetables, especially hot or cold artichokes.

FIVE P.M. TREAT

2 c. cheddar cheese, grated
1 c. green onion, sliced
1 c. olives, chopped
½ c. salsa
French bread rolls

1. Mix ingredients.
2. Spread onto thinly sliced rolls.
3. Place in broiler until bubbly.
4. Serve.

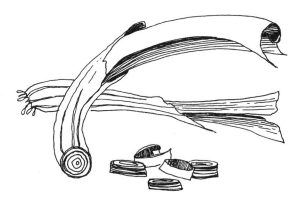

GREAT POTATO PANCAKES

6 potatoes, peeled
½ onion, grated
4 egg-yolks, beaten
Sea salt, to taste
Oil (corn or peanut)

1. Grate 6 potatoes into a bowl.
2. Over sink, squeeze out as much juice as possible.
3. Put back into bowl, add 4 beaten egg yokes and sea salt to taste.
4. On griddle or in fry pan, heat oil until it is sizzling.
5. Make potato mixture into patties and squeeze juice out over sink again.
6. Put on griddle, brown on both sides, and put on brown paper bag or napkin to drain.

Delicious hot or cold with meals or alone. Can be served with apple sauce or sour cream.

GUACAMOLE

Into a blender or food processor add the following ingredients in proportions to your liking:

Avocados
Salsa
Green onions, chopped
Tomatoes, chopped
Garlic powder
Lemon juice
Coriander
Sea salt

Blend and serve.

HERB-STUFFED EGGS

6 eggs, hard boiled
¼ c. yogurt
1 T. chopped parsley
¼ t. marjoram
Sea salt to taste
Toasted sesame seeds

1. Hard boil eggs.
2. Cut lengthwise and remove yolks.
3. Put yolks into a bowl and add yogurt, parsley, marjoram, and sea salt to taste.
4. Mash with a fork until mixed well but not runny.
5. Scoop into egg-white halves and cover with toasted sesame seeds.

For variations, add mayonnaise or sour cream instead of yogurt. Try dill and lemon juice or curry and cayenne. Experiment and make up your own variations.

LATE-NIGHT MUNCHY

1 chapati (whole wheat) or whole wheat tortilla per person
3 T. cottage cheese
1-2 t. mayonnaise
½ small avocado
¼ red onion, diced
Handful of alfalfa sprouts
Protein seasoning

1. Toast chapati in toaster, or over gas burner.
2. Mix all ingredients, wrap in chapati and eat.

Serves 1.

PABINI'S YUMMY WAY TO TAKE BREWER'S YEAST

1 c. sesami butter or tahini
2 c. almond butter, ground almonds, or almond meal
4 c. Brewer's yeast
⅛ c. olive oil
1 T. paprika
1 T. caraway powder
2 T. Dr. Bronner's liquid bouillon (or tamari, or soy sauce)
2 T. Dr. Jensen's seasoning or VegeSal
1 c. water
1 c. parsley, chopped

1. Combine all ingredients in shallow baking dish or casserole pan.
2. Refrigerate, cut in squares, and eat daily.

Tastes great also on a lettuce salad, in a sandwich, or by itself.

POTATO PUFFS

Russet potatoes
Bread crumbs
Melted butter

1. Preheat oven to 400°.
2. Peel potatoes and slice into ½″ pieces.
3. Dip in melted butter and roll in bread crumbs.
4. Place on ungreased cookie sheet and bake in pre-heated oven until soft, approximately 30-45 minutes.

Dip in sour cream for a real treat!

ROQUEFORT DRESSING OR DIP (Cheeseless)

1 lb. tofu
1 c. nutritional yeast
½ c. white miso
1 c. soy whey or water
2 T. Spike seasoning
1 t. mustard (wet)
2 t. garlic powder
2 T. apple cider vinegar
¼ c. olive oil
1 T. dill
2 T. soy sauce
1 T. white wine (optional)

1. Blend all ingredients except dill.
2. After well blended, stir in dill.
3. Add more vinegar, oil, and liquid if you want it to pour.

SHRIMP CANAPES

12 2-inch squares of whole wheat bread, toasted
½ lb. cooked shrimp (small)
1 green onion, minced
½ c. yogurt, plain
½ t. garlic granules
½ t. tamari
2 large avocados
Juice of ½ lemon
Paprika
Lemon slices
Parsley

1. Blend avocado and all ingredients except shrimp.
2. Spread onto bread squares, then sprinkle with shrimp and paprika.
3. Garnish with lemon slices and parsley.
4. Serve.

SNOW CAPS

2-3 dozen large mushrooms
1 c. cooked couscous
1 bunch green onions, finely chopped
2 carrots, finely chopped
2 T. mayonnaise
1 pkg. Gouda cheese (preferably with car-
    away seeds)
½ t. garlic powder
½ t. Italian seasoning
¼ stick butter
Juice of ½ lemon
VegeSal to taste
Paprika, sprinkled to taste

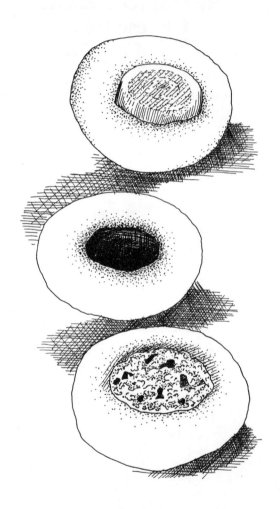

1. Preheat oven to 375°.
2. Cook couscous.
3. Add green onions, carrots, mayonnaise, and butter to couscous, and mix
   well.
4. Add seasonings and lemon.
5. Chop Gouda cheese into small squares
   and place inside washed and de-
   stemmed mushrooms, and place on
   cookie sheet.
6. Cover de-stemmed caps with couscous
   mixture, sprinkle with paprika, and
   bake until lightly brown.

STUFFED MUSHROOMS

1½ c. cooked buckwheat groats
1 c. soybean spread, or other cooked beans
  or bean-dip
3 t. VegeSal
1 T. onion, minced
2 T. sunflower seeds
¾ c. Muenster cheese, grated

1. Mix all ingredients together, except the cheese.
2. Stuff into mushroom caps (on cookie sheet), sprinkle with grated cheese, and bake in 350° oven until warm and browned.

TOFU CURRY DIP

½ lb. (2 large pieces) tofu, rinsed
1 fresh tomato, chopped
1 t. Dijon mustard
1 t. curry powder
1 t. garlic powder
¼-½ c. yogurt
Pinch cayenne or few drops tabasco sauce

1. Mix all ingredients in blender with enough yogurt to moisten.
2. Serve with crackers or raw vegetables.

Prepare the day before or early in the day for that evening.

BREADS AND MUFFINS

A & B MUFFINS

1 c. whole wheat flour
2 c. bran
2 T. baking powder
1 t. salt
2 t. cinnamon
½ t. nutmeg
½ c. sesame seeds
2 eggs
¼ c. melted butter
⅓ c. honey
⅔ c. buttermilk (or milk)
2 medium apples, grated

1. Pre-heat oven to 375°.
2. Mix whole wheat flour, bran, baking powder, salt, cinnamon, nutmeg, and sesame seeds.
3. In a separate bowl, mix eggs, melted butter, honey, buttermilk (or milk), and grated apples.
4. Mix all ingredients together and place in well-greased muffin tin.
5. Bake 25 minutes.

Makes 12 muffins.

BEST BANANA BREAD

1 c. unbleached white flour
1 c. whole wheat flour
1 T. baking powder
1 T. cinnamon
½ t. nutmeg
½ t. cloves
½ c. sunflower seeds or nuts
½ c. coconut, grated
2 eggs
2 t. vanilla
½ c. melted butter
½ c. honey
5-6 medium bananas, peeled and mashed

1. Mix dry ingredients and wet ingredients in separate bowls.
2. Add alternately dry and wet ingredients into 3 small (or 1 large) greased bread pans.
3. Bake at 325° for 45-50 minutes.

BEST BRAN MUFFINS

1 c. whole wheat flour
¼ c. soy flour
¼ c. powdered milk
3 t. baking powder
1 t. salt
1 c. whole bran
½-1 c. fresh walnut pieces
¼ c. melted butter
⅓-½ c. honey
2 eggs
1 c. milk

1. Pre-heat oven to 400°.
2. Mix whole wheat flour, soy flour, pow-dered milk, baking powder, salt, whole bran, and walnut pieces in a bowl.
3. In a separate bowl, mix butter, honey, eggs, and milk.
4. Mix all ingredients together and bake in greased muffin pan until browned and cooked through.

Yields 12 muffins.

BLUEBERRY MUFFINS

2 c. whole wheat flour
4 t. baking powder
¼ t. baking soda
¼ t. salt
2 eggs
½ c. milk
1 c. blueberry yogurt
1 c. blueberries (frozen will do)
¼ c. butter
½ c. honey

1. Pre-heat oven to 350°.
2. Mix and pour into greased muffin tin.
3. Bake at 350° for 40 minutes.

BRAN ENGLISH MUFFINS

4 c. whole wheat flour
2 pkg. active dry yeast
½ c. bran flakes
½ c. cracked wheat
¼ c. wheat germ
2 c. milk
¼ c. butter
1 T. honey
1 T. molasses
2 t. salt
Cornmeal

1. Combine yeast, ¾ c. flour, bran, cracked wheat, and wheat germ in large bowl.
2. In pan, heat milk, butter, honey, molasses, and salt until shortening almost melts. Add to dry ingredients, above.
3. Beat mixture ½ minute on low and 3 minutes on high. Stir in enough remaining flour to make a moderately stiff dough and knead on floured board for 10 minutes.
4. Place in greased bowl and let rise 1¼ hours.
5. Knead and let rise again 10 minutes.
6. Roll into ½"-thickness and cut into 4"-circles. Use a large glass or bowl as a punch. Dip both sides in cornmeal and cover. Let rise for 30 minutes.
7. Cook on ungreased griddle 25-28 minutes (or until golden brown), turning frequently.

This is quite time-consuming, but well worth the effort.

CORNBREAD

1 c. whole wheat flour
¼ c. honey
4 t. baking powder
¾ t. salt
1 c. cornmeal
2 eggs
1 c. buttermilk
¼ c. oil

1. Pre-heat oven to 350°.
2. Combine all ingredients in muffin tin.
3. Bake for 40 minutes.

CORNBREAD MUFFINS

1 c. whole wheat flour
¼ c. brown sugar
4 t. baking powder
¾ t. salt
1 c. corn meal
2 eggs
1 c. buttermilk
¼ c. oil

1. Pre-heat oven to 350°.
2. Mix all ingredients and place into greased muffin tin.
3. Bake at 350° for 40 minutes.

Good with chicken dishes.

CRUNCHY CORNBREAD

1 c. corn meal
½ c. whole wheat flour
½ c. wheat germ
¼ c. sesame seeds
2 T. baking powder
½ t. salt
¼ c. honey
1 egg
¼ c. milk or buttermilk

1. Pre-heat oven to 350°.
2. Mix together first 6 ingredients listed above: corn meal, whole wheat flour, wheat germ, sesame seeds, baking powder, and salt.
3. In a separate bowl, mix last 3 ingredients: honey, egg, and milk or buttermilk.
4. Mix all ingredients together and place in greased pan.
5. Bake ½ hour.

DIANE'S COTTAGE CHEESE & RAISIN BREAD

2 c. whole wheat flour
4 t. baking powder
¼ t. baking soda
¼ t. salt
1 t. caraway seeds
½ c. raisins
½ c. milk
¼ c. butter
¼ c. honey
1 c. cottage cheese
¼ c. wheat germ

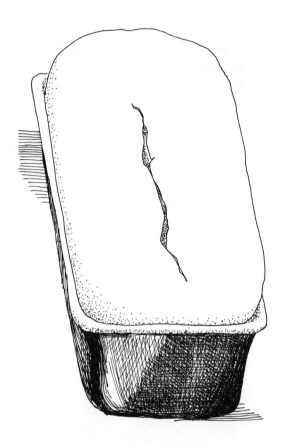

1. Pre-heat oven to 375°.
2. Mix all ingredients together and pour into greased pan or round baking dish.
3. Bake at 375° for 10 minutes, then lower oven to 350° and bake for 40 minutes.

A special treat heated for breakfast.

GREAT BREAD

2½ c. milk
4 T. honey
2 T. molasses
4 T. safflower oil
2 T. lecithin
⅔ c. whole wheat flour
2 T. salt
½ c. sesame seeds
½ c. soy flour
1 egg
3½ c. whole wheat flour

1. Pre-heat oven to 350°.
2. Mix first 5 ingredients above: milk, honey, molasses, safflower oil, and lecithin. Heat slightly.
3. Add ⅔ c. whole wheat flour and let rise.
4. After the above has risen, add salt, sesame seeds, soy flour, egg, and 3½ c. whole wheat flour.
5. Let rise once in bread pan.
6. Brush with egg white and water and bake 45-50 minutes.

MARYANNE'S QUICK HONEY BREAD

2 c. whole wheat flour
1 t. baking powder
1 t. baking soda
1 t. salt
½ t. cinnamon
½ t. ginger
½ c. honey
1 egg, slightly beaten
1 c. milk (or buttermilk)

1. Pre-heat oven to 350°.
2. Grease one 9"-×-5" baking pan or bread pan.
3. Combine all ingredients, pouring into baking pan, and bake for 50 minutes.

Easy and delicious served warm. Great for company — never fails.

QUICK WHOLE WHEAT BREAD

1 c. enriched white flour
½ c. whole wheat flour
1½ t. salt
2 pkg. yeast
½ c. water
1 c. milk
½-¾ c. honey
½ c. oil
2 T. molasses
2 eggs
1 c. enriched white flour
2 c. whole wheat flour

1. Pre-heat oven to 375°; mix first 4 ingredients above.
2. In a saucepan, heat water, milk, honey, oil, and molasses until very warm.
3. Add eggs and heated liquid to first 4 dry ingredients.
4. Blend at low speed, then beat for 3 minutes.
5. Stir in eggs and flours.
6. Cover, let rise in *warm* place about 50 minutes.
7. Stir down. Spoon into greased pans.
8. Bake at 375° for 30-35 minutes.

RUTH'S RYE BREAD

2 c. warm water, or chicken or vegetable stock
3 T. molasses
2 T. honey
2 T. oil
2 T. dry yeast
2 c. whole wheat flour
2 c. rye flour
2 t. salt
1 T. caraway seeds
½ c. gluten flour

1. Combine first 5 ingredients; let yeast foam and rise for 10 minutes.
2. Mix 2 c. whole wheat flour with 1 c. rye flour.
3. Add flour to yeast mixture and beat well about 100 times to form a spongy texture. Let rise and rest (cover with towel) in a warm place for approximately ½ hour.
4. Add salt, caraway seeds, gluten flour, and the rest of the rye flour.
5. Knead well, adding more gluten flour to breadboard as needed to keep hands from sticking to bread.
6. Let rise 45 minutes, covered in an oiled bowl in a warm place. Knead down and shape into 2 loaves.
7. Place in oiled bread pans and let rise another 45 minutes, or until level with top of pans.
8. Bake at 350° for 40-45 minutes.

Yields 2 loaves.

Tastes great toasted.

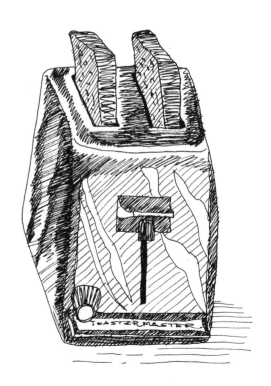

SPECIAL GARLIC TOAST

1 c. mayonnaise
½ c. Parmesan cheese
2 T. oil
2 t. paprika
1 clove garlic, crushed
1 round sesame Italian bread
Butter

1. Cut bread in half, butter, and broil until brown.
2. Spread with above ingredients blended into a paste.
3. Put bread back together, wrap in foil, and bake at 350° for 20 minutes.
4. Open and broil for 3 minutes.

SUPER MOIST BANANA BREAD

½ c. brown sugar
¼ c. honey
1 egg
1 c. whole wheat pastry flour
½ c. enriched white flour
½ c. butter
1 t. baking soda
½ t. sea salt
¼ c. yogurt
3 medium-sized, overripe bananas
¼ c. coconut or poppy seeds
1 c. walnuts or pecans (optional)

1. Pre-heat oven to 350°.
2. Cream egg, butter, honey, and brown sugar.
3. Sift together flour, soda, and salt, and combine with yogurt.
4. Mash bananas and add to flour mixture.
5. Combine all ingredients and mix lightly.
6. Pour into well-buttered bread pan.
7. Sprinkle top with coconut.
8. Bake for 50-60 minutes (or until golden brown). Do not overbake; keep moist but not wet.

Yields one loaf.

Special treat: When bread comes out of oven, cool slightly. Smooth honey over top and sprinkle with poppy seeds. Super! A great gift bread.

YOGURT DILL BREAD

2 c. whole wheat flour
4 t. baking powder
¼ t. baking soda
¼ t. salt
1 t. caraway seeds
1 t. dill
½ c. milk
¼ c. butter
¼ c. honey
1 c. yogurt
¼ c. wheat germ

1. Pre-heat oven to 375°.
2. Mix all ingredients together and pour into greased bread pan or round baking dish.
3. Bake at 375° for 10 minutes, then lower oven to 350° and bake for 40 minutes.

Moist and delicious.

THE MAIN COURSE & ACCESSORIES

ARTICHOKE-HEART CASSEROLE

1½ c. whole wheat noodles
1 onion, diced
1 c. mushrooms, chopped
2 pkgs. frozen artichoke hearts
2 cans Cheddar Cheese soup
½ c. milk
2 T. Jensen's seasoning
1 c. Jack cheese, grated
Pepper
Italian seasoning
Bread crumbs
Balanced almond mix
Paprika
Butter

1. Pre-heat oven to 425°.
2. Boil whole wheat noodles in enough water to cover them.
3. Sauté onion and mushrooms in butter.
4. Cook artichoke hearts as directed on package.
5. Heat Cheddar Cheese soup, adding milk, Jensen's seasoning, pepper, Italian seasoning, and grated Jack cheese.
6. Pour noodles into large casserole dish. Add sautéed vegetables and artichoke hearts. Cover with cheese sauce and mix together.
7. Add bread crumbs and balanced almond mix. Top with paprika, almonds, and bread crumbs.
8. Bake at 400° for approximately 20 minutes, until brown and bubbling.

Serves about 6.

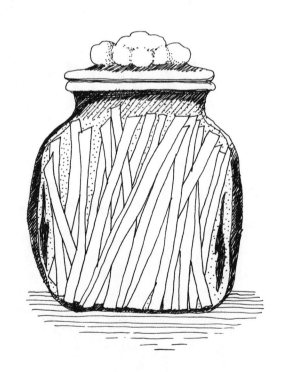

ASPARAGUS PARMESAN

1 c. bulgur cooked in 2 c. water
1 bunch asparagus, with bottoms trimmed off
1 yellow onion, chopped
1 large zucchini, sliced
Parmesan cheese, grated very fine or powdered
Butter
Garlic powder
Sea salt
Italian seasoning

1. Cook bulgur wheat.
2. Sauté the asparagus, onion, and zucchini in a lot of butter and garlic; add sea salt and Italian seasoning.
3. Pour mixture over bulgur and smother with Parmesan cheese.

Serves 2-4.

Good side dish.

BAKED FILET OF SOLE WITH WHITE SAUCE

2 lb. filet of sole
1 large container Ricotta cheese
½ lb. Jack cheese
½ t. garlic granules
1 t. tamari
½ t. sea salt
2 T. white wine
Juice of 1 lemon
Parsley flakes
Paprika

1. Pre-heat oven to 400°.
2. Grease or line a large baking dish. Place filets in dish.
3. Mix together in a bowl, Ricotta cheese, lemon juice, garlic, tamari, and sea salt, along with white wine.
4. Cover fish with mixture. Across the top, sprinkle with grated cheese, parsley, and paprika.
5. Bake at 400° for 20-25 minutes, until fish is flaky.

A good recipe to please the whole family.

BARBARA'S RED SNAPPER CASSEROLE

2 red snapper filets, approximately 1 lb.
1 can stewed tomatoes (16 oz.)
½ pt. sour cream
1 yellow onion, diced
2 sprigs parsley, chopped
½ c. peas or corn
½ c. Jack cheese, grated
1 c. mushrooms, sliced

1. Pre-heat oven to 350°.
2. Mix all ingredients except fish and cheese in saucepan.
3. Simmer 20-30 minutes.
4. Place fish in glass or stainless steel pan and cover with sauce; top with grated cheese.
5. Bake for 30 minutes and serve over rice.

Serves 2.

Sole or sea bass may be substituted for snapper.

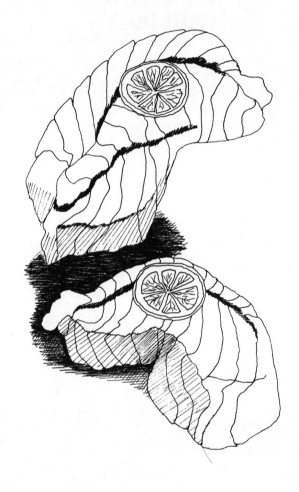

BLENDED SPINACH PIE

Filling:

1 large onion, chopped
2 stalks celery, chopped
2 eggs
¾ c. milk (or half & half)
4 oz. Ricotta cheese
2 oz. sour cream
1 oz. Jack cheese, grated
1 large bunch spinach, chopped
2 t. Jensen's seasoning or VegeSal
Butter
Sea salt
Garlic granules

Crust:

1 T. sour cream
½ c. oil
¾-1 c. whole wheat flour
¾ c. almonds, crushed or ground
2 T. tahini or sesame butter
Water

1. Pre-heat oven to 375°.
2. Combine crust ingredients and press into large pie pan. Bake 5-7 minutes.
3. Sauté the chopped onion, celery, and spinach in butter, heavily laced with garlic.
4. Combine in blender the eggs, milk, Ricotta cheese, sour cream, Jack cheese, sautéed vegetables, and seasoning. Blend at medium speed until smooth.
5. Top with seeds and paprika. Bake 25-30 minutes, until fluffy, warm and brown.

Serves 4-6.

Colorful and delicious.

BOUILLABAISSE

¼ c. olive oil
1 stalk celery, chopped
1 medium onion, chopped
1 clove garlic, chopped
1 leek, chopped
½ t. thyme
1 bay leaf
2 c. crushed tomatoes
1 c. clam juice (bottled)
1 c. dry white wine
½ t. crushed fennel
2 T. parsley, chopped
1 small lobster tail, or crab
12 clams
1 lb. cleaned shrimp
12 scallops
1 lb. firm fish (snapper or bass)
Pinch or saffron
Salt and pepper

1. In large pot, cook vegetables in oil at medium heat for 5 minutes.
2. Add tomatoes, liquids, and spices, and simmer for 15 minutes.
3. Add clams and cook 10 minutes more.
4. Add remaining fish and cook 15 minutes longer.

Serve in bowls. Earthenware or clay pottery bowls retain warmth and are attractive.

BROCCOLI NOODLE PIE

1 small pkg. whole wheat noodles
1 bunch fresh broccoli, cut into bite-sized
  chunks
8 oz. Ricotta cheese
1 tofu cake
½ t. Italian seasoning
½ yellow onion, chopped
¼ lb. mushrooms, sliced
2 cans tomato sauce (or 12-16 oz. freshly
made)
Parmesan cheese
Garlic powder to taste

1. Pre-heat oven to 400°.
2. Cook noodles as directed on package.
3. Cut and lightly steam broccoli.
4. Mix Ricotta cheese, tofu, and seasonings.
5. Heat tomato sauce with onions and mushrooms. Simmer 15 minutes.
6. Rinse noodles and line baking dish with half of the noodles. Add half of the broccoli and cheese mixture, and pour half of the tomato sauce over.
7. Cover remaining noodles with rest of cheese mixture and sauce. Sprinkle Parmesan cheese over top.
8. Bake until brown and bubbling, approximately 15-20 minutes.

Serves 4.

Delicious!

BROCCOLI PIE

1 large yellow onion, chopped
1 bunch broccoli, chopped
3 eggs
1 c. milk
8 oz. cream cheese
½ c. Parmesan cheese
1 t. garlic powder
½ t. Italian seasoning
½ t. sea salt
Butter

1. Pre-heat oven to 375°.
2. Sauté chopped onion and broccoli in butter, until soft but crunchy.
3. Combine in blender the eggs, milk, cream cheese, Parmesan, and seasonings.
4. Pour all into baking dish (large pyrex pie pan is great), and bake for approximately 30 minutes.

Serves 3-4.

BULGUR WHEAT YUMMY

1 c. uncooked bulgur wheat
¼ c. milk
4 oz. Ricotta cheese
2 oz. cottage cheese
2-3 T. tamari
¼ c. sunflower seeds
1 sprig parsley, chopped
2 c. water

1. Cook bulgur with 2 c. water: boil water, add bulgur, cover and simmer until all water is gone and grain is tender.
2. Add Ricotta, cottage cheese, milk, and tamari until well blended.
3. Mix in parsley and sunflower seeds.

Serves 4.

Serve hot or cold.

BUTTERFISH MACADAMIA CASSEROLE

1 T. whole wheat flour
¾-1 lb. butterfish, chopped into bite-sized
   pieces
1 c. rice, cooked with 2 c. water
1 zucchini, sliced
1 bunch green onions, chopped
½ lb. mushrooms, sliced
¾ lb. Jack cheese, grated
2 carrots, sliced
1 c. cottage cheese
½ c. milk
4 oz. macadamia nuts
Garlic to taste

1. Sauté the garlic, zucchini, onion,
   mushrooms, and carrots in butter.
2. In blender, blend flour, cottage cheese,
   milk, and cheese, and add the drained,
   sautéed vegetables. Blend again.
3. Mix cooked rice, fish, and blended
   sauce in deep-dish casserole. Top with
   chopped nuts.
4. Bake at 350° for 30 minutes.

Serves 4.

A special treat for special occasions.

CALIFORNIA QUICHE

1 lb. zucchini
2 c. cheese (1 c. grated cheese, 1 c. cottage
cheese)
4 eggs
½ onion, diced
½ t. each basil, oregano, and pepper
¼ lb. mushrooms, chopped or sliced
¼ c. Baco-Bits

1. Pre-heat oven to 325°.
2. Steam zucchini and onion. Mash and
   add to blended eggs, cheese, and seasoning. Stir in mushrooms and Baco-
   Bits. Pour into prepared whole wheat
   crust.
3. Cover and bake for 40 minutes.

Serves 4-5.

CARAWAY BROCCOLI CUSTARD

1 bunch broccoli, steamed lightly
2 T. sour cream
1 T. cottage cheese
4 oz. milk
4 oz. Jack or Cheddar cheese, grated
1 egg
2 t. Jensen's seasoning (or VegeSal)
½ clove garlic
¾ t. caraway powder
¼ c. sesame seeds
⅛-¼ c. caraway seeds
Juice of ½ lemon

1. Pre-heat oven to 375°.
2. Steam broccoli.
3. Mix sour cream, cottage cheese, milk, lemon juice, and seasonings in blender at medium speed.
4. In baking dish, combine broccoli, blended ingredients, caraway seeds, and sesame. Top with cheese.
5. Bake approximately 30 minutes.

Serves 3-4.

May also be served over rice or noodles.

CAULIFLOWER PIE

1 small cauliflower, chopped
½ red onion, chopped
½ c. milk (or half & half)
4 oz. sour cream
4 oz. cottage cheese
1 tofu cake
3 green onions, chopped
2-3 stalks celery, chopped
2 t. Jensen's seasoning (or VegeSal)
½ t. Italian seasoning
½ t. garlic salt
1 t. tamari
¼ c. wheat germ
1 c. cooked brown rice (may be leftover)

1. Pre-heat oven to 375°.
2. Steam or sauté cauliflower, red onion, and celery.
3. Combine sour cream, cottage cheese, and tofu. Blend with milk and seasoning.
4. Pour mixture into pyrex baking dish. Add vegetables, green onions, wheat germ, and rice to casserole.
5. Bake 25-35 minutes, until brown.

Serves 3-4.

CHAPATI TOSTADA

1 tofu cake
6 oz. soybean spread, cooked beans, or bean dip
1 avocado
½ c. alfalfa sprouts
1 c. cooked buckwheat groats
2 t. Jensen's seasoning (or VegeSal)
1 head of lettuce, shreaded
3 carrots, grated
2 tomatoes, chopped
1 small carton sour cream
1 c. grated cheddar cheese
Hot sauce (optional)
Whole wheat tortillas or chapatis
Oil

1. Mix tofu, bean spread, avocado, sprouts, and cooked buckwheat together; season to taste.
2. Coat whole wheat chapatis (or tortillas) with oil, add Jensen's, and bake at 375° for 5-8 minutes.
3. Remove from oven and spread with above mixture.
4. Cover with lettuce, carrots, sprouts, tomatoes, sour cream, and cheese. Add hot sauce if you wish. Can be eaten hot or cold.

Serves 4.

A sauce of olive oil, garlic salt, and Jensen's seasoning tops it off nicely.

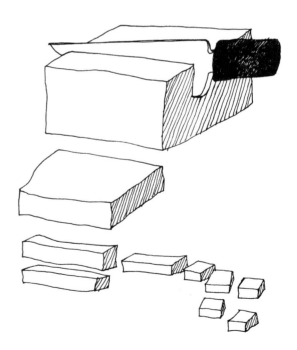

CHEESE & VEGETABLE PIE
(The J&D Special)

½ yellow onion, chopped
1 T. oil
2 c. broccoli, chopped
1 c. mushrooms, chopped
1 c. Jack cheese, shredded
2 t. salt
¼ t. pepper
½ t. oregano
1½ c. whole wheat flour
1½ c. milk
½ c. walnuts
3 eggs

1. Pre-heat oven to 400°.
2. Sauté onion, broccoli, mushrooms, and nuts in oil.
3. Mix together the salt, pepper, oregano, whole wheat flour, milk, and eggs.
4. Pour half the flour mixture in rectangular casserole dish; place vegetables on top, cover with cheese, and pour second half flour mixture over top.
5. Bake for 45-60 minutes.

Serves 4-6.

CHEESE SOUFFLE

1 c. milk
¼ c. powdered milk
3 T. unbleached flour
1½ t. sea salt
⅛ t. pepper
½ t. cream of tartar
¼ t. basil
5 eggs
1½ c. Cheddar cheese, shredded
2-3 T. chopped parsley
Butter

1. Pre-heat oven to 300°.
2. Heat 1 c. milk to simmer.
3. Blend powdered milk, unbleached white flour, salt, pepper, and basil.
4. Add to hot milk and cook over medium heat, stirring with wisk until sauce thickens.
5. Remove from heat and cool a bit. Add 4 egg yolks, shredded Cheddar cheese and chopped parsley.
6. Beat 5 egg whites until stiff. Add salt, cream of tartar, and fold into sauce.
7. Pour into well-buttered deep casserole dish. Bake at 300° for 1 hour.

Great for special occasions. Looks especially nice served in earthenware or decorative pottery.

CHEESE 'N SOY ENCHILADA

2 cartons soy spread (or 12 oz. cooked beans or bean dip).
2 carrots, grated
2 avocados
1 c. caraway Muenster cheese, grated
¾ c. alfalfa sprouts
1 t. garlic powder
½ t. pepper
Jensen's seasoning (or VegeSal) to taste

1. Mix all above ingredients together.
2. Pre-heat oven to 400°.
3. Take whole wheat tortilla and rub with safflower oil and sprinkle with garlic powder.
4. Fill with mixture, roll up and tuck in ends. (May be topped with grated cheese or tomato sauce.)
5. Place in baking pan.
6. Bake at 400° approximately 10 minutes, or until heated through.

Serves 4-6.

Spanish millet complements this dish beautifully.

CHEESELESS WHOLE WHEAT PIZZA

Crust:

1 c. whole wheat flour
½ c. buckwheat flour
1 T. oil
½ c. warm water
1½ t. active dry yeast

Pizza topping:

2 small tofu cakes, mashed
1 onion, thinly sliced
Mushrooms, sliced
Green pepper, chopped
Tomato sauce

1. Dissolve yeast in warm water; then stir in oil and flour.
2. Cover breadboard lightly with flour and knead mixture until smooth.
3. Place kneaded ball in greased container, cover and let rise 40-45 minutes.
4. Pre-heat oven to 450°.
5. Spread dough over well-greased pizza pan or equivalent and bake 8-10 minutes.
6. Add topping, pour sauce over and top with tofu.
7. Bake until brown (less than 5 minutes).

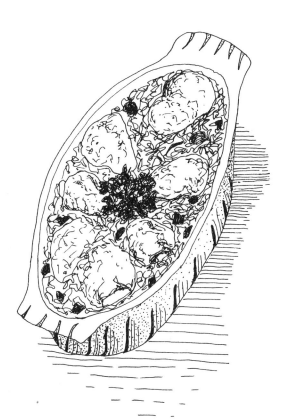

CHICKEN MARENGO

2 c. cooked chicken pieces
2 onions, chopped
2 cloves garlic, minced
2 T. butter or oil
1 can tomatoes, cut up and drained
1 green pepper, chopped
1 c. mushrooms, sliced
1 c. white wine
½ c. olives, sliced
1 t. Italian seasoning

1. Sauté onions and garlic in butter.
2. Add tomatoes, green pepper, mushrooms, olives, Italian seasoning, and wine. Simmer until glazed.
3. Add pieces of cooked chicken. Heat thoroughly.

Serves 3-4.

Serve over rice.

CHICKEN PEACHES

4 chicken breasts
1 large can peaches and juice
¼ c. Worchestershire sauce
½ t. cinnamon
1 T. cornstarch
1 T. water
½ c. butter
salt and pepper

1. Cut chicken meat into large bite-sized chunks. Discard skin and bones.
2. Sauté chicken in butter, salt and pepper for 15 minutes.
3. Add peaches, juice, Worchestershire sauce, and cinnamon. Sauté for 30 minutes.
4. Add cornstarch dissolved in water. Boil until thick.

Serves 4.

Serve over rice pilaf.

CREAMY SHRIMP-ASPARAGUS QUICHE

Filling:

3 eggs, beaten
1 c. cream, scalded
½ lb. each Jack and Cheddar cheeses, grated
½ lb. fresh shrimp
1 bunch asparagus, sautéed in butter and garlic

Crust:

⅔-1 c. whole wheat flour
¼ c. oil
¾-1 c. butter
⅛ c. Parmesan cheese

1. Pre-heat oven to 400°.
2. Mix crust ingredients and pat into pan. Bake 5-10 minutes.
3. Mix eggs and cream, and pour into crust with asparagus.
4. Bake for approximately 25-30 minutes, until firm.

Serves 4-6.

An impressive main course for special occasions.

CREAMY SPICED CHICKEN OVER COUSCOUS

2 pkg. boned chicken parts
1 green pepper, chopped
2 carrots, chopped
1 red pepper, chopped
1 c. bean sprouts
2 t. curry
1 t. garlic
½ t. cumin
1 t. cayenne
1 T. parsley flakes
2 T. tamari
Butter
Garlic
Large carton yogurt or sour cream

1. Cut chicken into bite-sized pieces.
2. Sauté in large skillet or frying pan in butter and garlic. (Some fresh ginger adds a spicy flavor.)
3. Add green pepper, carrots, and red pepper, and sauté until chicken is tender.
4. Add seasoning, sour cream, and bean sprouts, and simmer until hot.
5. Cook couscous as directed on package (or see Grain section).
6. Pour mixture over couscous and serve.

Serves 4.

A family favorite.

CURRIED CHICKEN

1 3-lb. chicken
1 T. oil
¾ c. sliced mushrooms
2 cloves garlic
½ onion, chopped
1 t. ginger
1½ t. curry
1 t. cumin
1½ t. sea salt
¼ t. cayenne pepper
1 c. yogurt

1. Pre-heat oven to 350°.
2. Place chicken in baking pan. Pour melted butter over chicken, cook 45 minutes, and remove from oven.
3. In wok or frying pan, combine oil with sliced mushrooms, minced garlic, chopped onion, ginger, curry, cumin, sea salt, and cayenne pepper, and sauté.
4. Add yogurt to above ingredients, pour over chicken and bake for approximately 15 minutes.

Serves 3-4.

Serve over rice.

CURRIED RICE

2 cloves garlic, minced
1 t. ginger
1 t. curry
1 t. sea salt
½ c. yogurt
1 T. oil
½ onion, chopped
2 stalks celery, chopped
1 t. cumin
Sprinkle cayenne pepper

1. Cook rice as directed (2 c. water to 1 c. rice) in fairly large saucepan. Cover.
2. In a wok or frying pan, combine all ingredients except yogurt in 1 T. oil. Heat until browned.
3. Mix in the yogurt.
4. Add to rice mixture, cover and simmer over low flame about 10 minutes.

Serves 4.

DARRYL'S SUPER VEGGIE BURRITO

2 c. Japanese adzuki beans
1 c. brown rice, uncooked
8 tomatoes, cooked and mashed for sauce
2½ c. water
2-3 red hot peppers, chopped
1 medium onion, chopped
2-3 cloves garlic
1 t. chili powder
1 t. thyme
1 t. paprika
1 t. Spike
1 doz. tortilla shells

1. Soak beans overnight. Drain.
2. Combine above ingredients into a large sauce pan. Cook over medium to high heat until rice and beans are done, about 1 hour (beans will be tender).
3. Wrap in a warm flour tortilla.
4. Garnish with sliced tomatoes, alfalfa sprouts, lettuce, grated Monterey or Mozerella cheese, and sliced black olives.

DENISE'S BARLEY CASSEROLE

⅔ c. barley, cooked
⅓ c. rice, cooked
4 eggs
1½ c. cheese, grated
4 leaves of chard
1 head spinach, chopped
1 medium zucchini, chopped
¾ t. garlic granules
1 t. Tobasco
2 T. wheat germ

1. Pre-heat oven to 350°.
2. Combine all ingredients in casserole dish.
3. Cover with wheat germ and bake for approximately 35 minutes.

Serves 4-6.

EGGPLANT PARMESAN

2 cans tomato sauce
1 eggplant, peeled and sliced in ½"-thick
    slices
1 onion, chopped
1 c. mushrooms
1 carton cottage cheese
1 lb. Mozarella cheese, sliced thin
Parmesan cheese
Olive oil
Garlic granules
Butter

1. Pre-heat oven to 400°.
2. Stick eggplant with fork and rub with olive oil. Bake 10 minutes.
3. Sauté onion and mushrooms in butter with a little garlic.
4. Over each eggplant slice, place a scoop of cottage cheese and one large slice of Mozarella cheese.
5. Cover with onions and mushrooms.
6. Pour tomato sauce over slices.
7. Bake approximately 45 minutes (or until tender).

Serves 4-6.

FISH CASSEROLE

1 lb. filet of sole
2 carrots, thinly sliced
1 green pepper, finely chopped
½ c. bean sprouts
¼ lb. mushrooms, sliced
2 stalks broccoli, cut into bite-sized pieces
¼ c. walnuts
8 oz. cottage cheese
3⅛ c. raw milk
4 oz. cream cheese
1 t. Jensen's seasoning (or VegeSal)
1 t. sea salt
Garlic powder, to taste
Sprinkle of Italian seasoning

1. Pre-heat oven to 350°.
2. Butter casserole dish or deep pie pan.
3. Cut fish into bite-sized pieces and place in baking dish.
4. Steam all vegetables lightly.
5. Combine milk, cottage cheese, cream cheese, and seasonings in blender.
6. Place vegetables over fish and cover with blended sauce. Bake 20-25 minutes, or until brown.

Serves 2-3.

FOILED FISH

3 lb. bass or 2 lb. cod
2 T. flour
4 T. oil
1 clove garlic, crushed
½ large green pepper, thinly sliced
¼ lb. mushrooms, sliced
¼ c. white wine
1 tomato, diced
¼ c. tomato paste
1 T. lemon juice
½ c. olives, sliced
1 t. each minced parsley, tarragon, basil
Salt and pepper

1. Sprinkle fish with flour and seasonings.
2. Heat oil in skillet, add garlic, then fish. Brown for 2 minutes on each side. Place fish in center of foil.
3. Sauté in wine the pepper strips, mushrooms, olives, and tomatoes.
4. Add tomato paste and lemon juice.
5. Spoon sauce onto shallow baking pan.
6. Bake at 425° for 20 minutes.

Serves 4.

Serve over rice or spinach noodles.

FRESH TOMATO SAUCE

10-12 tomatoes, skinned*
2 onions, chopped
½-¾ lb. mushrooms, chopped
1 zucchini, chopped
2 cloves garlic
2 bay leaves
4 stalks celery, diced
1 T. basil
1 t. sea salt
½ t. pepper
2 T. tahini
2 T. tamari

1. Combine all ingredients, except tahini, in large kettle or stainless steel pot.
2. Bring to a boil, then simmer for 30-45 minutes. Add water if too thick.
3. Add tahini at end of cooking. May be kept overnight to enhance flavor.

The taste is worth the effort.

In a pot of boiling water, drop in a tomato until skin starts to wrinkle and peel. Take out and pull off the rest of the peel.

GENERAL QUICHE RECIPE

Filling:

3 eggs
½ c. milk
½ c. cream
½ pkg. Ricotta cheese or 1 c. grated cheese
¼ c. Parmesan cheese

Crust:

¾-1 c. whole wheat flour
1½ c. butter, melted
2 T. Parmesan cheese
2-4 t. water
Seasoning

1. Mix crust and put into pie shell.
2. Mix creamy ingredients and place in shell.
3. Grate Parmesan cheese on top and bake at 400° for approximately 25-30 minutes.
4. Add any of the following sautéed vegetables to the filling: onions, zucchini, mushrooms, or spinach.

Serves 4-6.

GINGER FISH

1 T. oil
1 lb. cod filets
½ c. green onions, sliced
1 c. mushrooms, sliced
1½ T. fresh ginger, grated
¼ c. vegetable or chicken stock
¼ c. white wine
4 t. tamari
1 T. cornstarch dissolved in 1 T. water
½ c. water chestnuts, sliced

1. Heat oil in wok or large frying pan, add fish and cook for 2 minutes. Turn fish.
2. Sprinkle onions, mushrooms, ginger, and water chestnuts over fish. Add wine and tamari.
3. Cover and let steam about 10 minutes, until flaky and tender.
4. Mix cornstarch and water, and gradually stir into hot liquid. Simmer a few minutes until thick.

Serves 2 generously.

Garnish with parsley and lemon slices and serve over brown rice.

JUDY'S QUICK CLAM SAUTE

1 lb. mushrooms, sliced
½ c. butter
2 cans minced clams, drained (let your kitty drink the juice)
3 cloves garlic, minced
1 T. Italian seasoning
Juice of 1 medium lemon
Spinach noodles
Parmesan cheese
Salt and pepper

1. Sauté sliced mushrooms in butter, then stir in rest of the ingredients.
2. Serve over spinach noodles and top with Parmesan cheese.

Serves 2-3.

All one needs to add is a green salad, garlic toast, white wine, and a candle for a romantic dinner.

LASAGNA VERDE

Noodle mixture:

1 pkg. lasagna noodles
16 oz. Ricotta cheese
¼ c. milk
16 oz. Mozarella cheese
1 lb. spinach
Parmesan cheese

Tomato sauce:

2 T. olive oil
4 cloves garlic, chopped
2 large onions, chopped
1 c. celery, sliced
1 carrot, grated
1 can tomato paste
2 qt. canned or fresh tomatoes (cooked)
1 c. tomato juice
2 t. sea salt
½-1 t. each oregano, thyme, marjoram, and basil
2 bay leaves, crumbled
½-1 lb. mushrooms, sliced
Water if necessary

1. Sauté in olive oil the garlic, onion, celery, and carrots.
2. Add tomato paste, canned tomatoes, tomato juice, salt and seasonings. Simmer on low heat for minimum of 1 hour, while preparing remainder of recipe.
3. Pre-heat oven to 350°.
4. Boil noodles and drain.
5. In bottom of baking dish, place one layer of noodles.
6. Whip Ricotta cheese with milk to thin. Wash, dry, and tear spinach into pieces.
7. Over layer of noodles, repeat with layers of cheeses, spinach, and sauce, ending with a layer of sauce topped with Parmesan cheese.
8. Bake for 20 minutes, until top is browned and sauce is bubbling.

Serves 8.

A vegetarian lasagna.

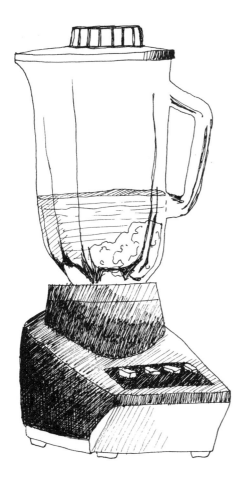

LOW-CALORIE MOCK WHITE SAUCE

(Cottage Cheese Sauce)

1 c. cottage cheese
½ c. milk
½ t. Italian seasoning
½ t. garlic salt
1 T. Jensen's seasoning

1. Place all ingredients in blender.
2. Mix at medium speed until creamy.

Tastes great over vegetables, fish, or salads. Low calorie, high protein.

MEATLESS MOUSSAKA

2 large potatoes, lightly boiled
1 large eggplant, sliced
2-3 T. olive oil
8 oz. Ricotta cheese
1-1½ c. Parmesan cheese, grated
1 t. paprika
1 t. oregano
½ t. thyme
1 t. garlic powder
1 t. salt
1 green pepper, chopped
1 large onion, chopped
1 small can tomato paste
6 oz. water
Juice of ½ lemon
Sprinkle cayenne pepper

1. Pre-heat oven to 400°.
2. Boil potatoes for about 20 minutes.
3. Cut the eggplant into ½″-slices. Place on cookie sheet rubbed with olive oil. Make a few holes in eggplant slices with fork and sprinkle each piece with a little oil. Bake for approximately 15-20 minutes, or until pieces are brown and soft. Lower oven to 350°.
4. Mash potatoes with a small amount of potato water, and add Ricotta cheese, ½ c. of the Parmesan cheese, the paprika, oregano, garlic, salt, and pepper.
5. Grease a baking dish and add sliced eggplant.
6. Sauté green pepper, onion, 2 T. olive oil, ½ t. garlic powder, 2 large pinches thyme, oregano, pepper, and 1 t. vegetable salt.
7. Add tomato paste, water, and lemon, cover and simmer for 10 minutes on low heat.
8. In baking pan, layer the eggplant, sauce, potatoes, and grated cheese. Make 2 layers and cover with more grated cheese.
9. Bake at 350°, uncovered, about 30 minutes, or until cooked throughout.

Serves 4.

MUSHROOM TOFU CASSEROLE

1¼ lb. mushrooms, sliced
1 large pkg. tofu
1 small carton raw cottage cheese
1 c. sunflower seeds
½ c. almonds, sliced
1 bunch green onions, chopped
½-1 c. raw milk
1 yellow onion, chopped
Jensen's seasoning or VegeSal
Garlic powder
Tamari
Paprika

1. Pre-heat oven to 425°.
2. Sauté yellow onion and mushrooms lightly in butter and garlic. Place in large casserole dish.
3. Add tofu, cottage cheese, seeds, almonds, milk, and tamari to taste.
4. Stir until mixture is loose but not runny. Make sure ingredients are mixed thoroughly. Keep adding milk if mixture is too thick.
5. Top with green onions and paprika.
6. Bake for about 35 minutes, until golden brown and bubbling.

Serves 4-6.

Also tastes good over rice or noodles.

ORIENTAL STYLE BROWN RICE

3 T. sesame oil
2 bunches scallions, chopped
1 clove garlic, finely chopped
4 ribs celery, diced
1 can water chestnuts, sliced
2 c. bean sprouts
3 T. parsley, chopped
1 t. oregano
½ t. basil
¾ c. sunflower seeds
2 T. fresh ginger, grated
½ c. honey
½ c. tamari (use less)
1 T. lemon juice
3 c. brown rice, cooked

1. Heat the oil in a wok or heavy iron skillet. Add scallions and cook quickly for 1 minute. Add garlic and celery and cook 1 minute.
2. Add water chestnuts, bean sprouts, and parsley; cook, stirring 1 minute. Stir in the oregano, basil, and sunflower seeds.
3. Combine the ginger, honey, soy sauce or tamari, and lemon juice, and stir into the vegetable mixture.
4. Stir in the cooked rice and reheat.

Serves 4-6.

PAT'S SPICY CASHEW CHICKEN

1 fryer chicken
¼ c. oil
1 onion, chopped
10 whole cloves of garlic
2 T. minced fresh ginger
1 stick cinnamon
2 whole cardamum
1 tomato, sliced
1 T. coriander, ground
1 T. coconut, shredded
1½ t. cumin, ground
¾ c. water
1 chicken bouillon cube
1 T. cashews, salted and roasted
Pinch saffron
Sea salt to taste

1. Pour ¼ c. salad oil into a heavy 12"-frying pan; place over medium-high heat.
2. Add 1 large chopped onion, 10 whole cloves of garlic, minced fresh ginger, stick of cinnamon, and 2 whole cardamum (shells removed). Cook, stirring until onion is browned, about 5 minutes.
3. Stir in ground coriander and shredded, unsweetened coconut. Add ground cumin.
4. Cut up fryer chicken and add to pot with water and chicken bouillon cube.
5. Cover and simmer about 45 minutes.
6. Stir into sauce a pinch of saffron. Add salted, roasted cashews and salt to taste.

Serves 3-4.

Garnish with fresh sliced tomatoes.

POTATO LOAF

2 cakes tofu, mashed
2 medium-sized potatoes
¼ c. almonds, ground
2 t. seasoning salt
½ loaf sprouted wheat bread (Wayfarers)
3 carrots, chopped
¼ c. milk
1 bunch spinach, steamed

1. Pre-heat oven to 375°.
2. Mix ground almonds with seasoning salt.
3. Steam or sauté potatoes and carrots. Mash together and add milk.
4. Line bottom of casserole dish with a layer of sprouted wheat bread and a layer of tofu.
5. Add potato-carrot mixture and steamed spinach.
6. Put another layer of tofu on top, cover with almonds, and bake at 375° until brown.

QUICK GUACAMOLE

3 avocados
½ t. garlic granules
1 small tomato, chopped
Juice of ½ lemon
Hot sauce, to taste

Combine ingredients in blender or food processor.

Serves 4.

RED SNAPPER IN CREAM SAUCE

1 lb. red snapper
½ lb. small shrimp
¼ lb. mushrooms, sliced
1 small carton cottage cheese
4 oz. cream cheese
½-¾ c. milk
1 t. Italian seasoning
1 bunch green onions
2 T. tamari
Juice of 1 small lemon
Paprika
Butter

1. Pre-heat oven to 400°.
2. Butter and bake snapper until about ¾ cooked.
3. Cover with more butter and sliced mushrooms.
4. Blend cottage cheese, cream cheese, milk, lemon juice, and seasoning. Pour over snapper.
5. Top with shrimp, paprika, and scallions.
6. Bake at 400° until tender, 15-20 minutes.

Serves 2.

RED SNAPPER SUPREME

1½ lbs. red snapper
2 T. olive oil
½ c. green pepper, chopped
½ c. celery, diced
½ c. onion, chopped
½ c. mushrooms, sliced
2-3 fresh tomatoes, chopped
1 T. fresh dry basil
½ t. thyme
½ t. sea salt
¼ c. red or white wine (optional)
1-2 T. whole wheat flour

1. Pre-heat oven to 375°.
2. Place snapper in oiled baking dish.
3. Sauté the green pepper in the olive oil; then add in order the celery, onion, mushrooms, and tomatoes. Add seasoning, wine, and flour; let simmer and thicken.
4. Pour sauce on top of fish and bake uncovered for 15 minutes, or until fish flakes easily.

Serves 3-4.

Suggestion: Serve on top of brown rice or spinach noodles.

SANDY'S QUICK TUNA CASSEROLE

3 cans cream of mushroom soup
2 onions, diced
3 cans milk (soup can)
1 large bag natural potato chips
2 large cans of tuna, packed in water

1. Pre-heat oven to 350°.
2. Heat soup, milk, and onions in a sauce pot.
3. Into a casserole dish, make a layer of potato chips, then a layer of tuna. Cover with soup sauce and repeat another layer. Pour the rest of the soup over the top.
4. Sprinkle with sunflower seeds, parsley flakes, and paprika.
5. Bake in 350° oven 25-30 minutes.

Serves 4-6.

Kids love it.

SHARONA'S GINGERED VEGETABLES WITH ORANGE SAUCE

Orange Sauce:

4 T. tamari (or soy sauce)
½ c. orange juice
¼ c. water
2 T. arrowroot powder (or corn starch)

Vegetables

4 T. soy oil
2-5 T. ginger root (to taste), freshly grated
2-4 cloves garlic (to taste), chopped or pressed
¾ c. carrots, chopped
¾ c. celery, diagonally sliced
¾ c. onion, chopped
1 green and/or sweet red pepper, chopped
1 c. mushrooms, sliced
¾ c. chinese cabbage, bok choy, or other type of greens, chopped
1 c. fresh snow pea pods (if available)
¾ c. bean sprouts
½ c. slivered almonds

1. Blend Orange Sauce ingredients together thoroughly until smooth.
2. Place oil in a wok (or the largest cast iron skillet you have) and heat over a medium-high flame. When thoroughly hot, add ginger, garlic, carrots, celery, and onion. Stir continuously for 2 minutes.
3. Add the peppers and mushrooms and stir for 1 minute.
4. Add the pea pods, stir for 2 minutes.
5. Add the greens and bean sprouts, blending the entire mixture well for 1 minute.
6. Fold in prepared orange sauce and stir lovingly for a minute or two.
7. Place in a serving dish and fold in the almonds. Now enjoy your savory delight!

For the quality of the dish to be maintained, it is essential that the ingredients not be overcooked. Cooking times given may be altered to fit your personal taste, however.

SOY SPREAD

1 c. soybeans, cooked
1 T. soy oil
1 green onion, chopped
½ t. Italian seasoning
¼ t. garlic
1 t. salt
2 T. tofu

1. Grind soybeans (or mash).
2. Mix all ingredients together.

This recipe may be used whenever soy spread is called for in this book.

SPANISH-STYLE MILLET

1 c. millet cooked with 2 c. water
1 can (12 oz.) tomato sauce
1 t. sea salt
3 green onions, chopped
¾ c. Cheddar cheese, grated
Hot sauce, to taste

1. Cook millet.
2. Add hot sauce, tomato sauce, onion, and seasoning salt.
3. Mix and top with grated cheese.

Serves 4.

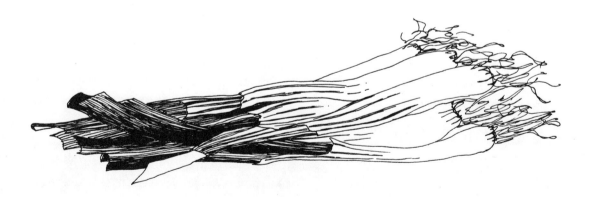

SPANISH-STYLE RICE

1 T. bulgur wheat
1 T. soy grits
10 oz. tomato juice
½ c. black olives, chopped
½ t. sea salt
1 T. barley
¾-1 c. brown rice
1 c. sharp Cheddar cheese, grated
½ t. black pepper

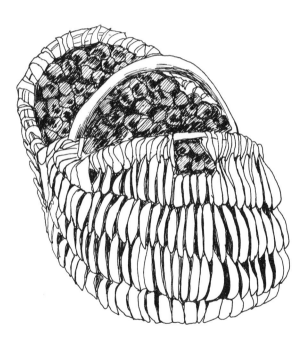

1. Into 1-cup measuring cup, add bulgur, barley, and soy grits, and fill to top with brown rice.
2. Cook with 2 c. water, as directed.
3. In a saucepan, combine tomato juice and seasoning, and pour over cooked rice.
4. Top with cheese and olives.

STUFFED FLOUNDER

¼ c. onion, chopped
¼ c. butter
1 3-oz. can mushrooms (save juice)
1 can crab meat (7½ oz.)
½ c. cracker crumbs
2 T. parsley, snipped
½ t. salt
2 lbs. flounder filets
3 T. butter
3 T. flour
¼ t. salt
⅓ c. dry white wine
1 c. (4 oz.) Swiss cheese, grated
½ t. paprika
Milk

1. Pre-heat oven to 400°.
2. Sauté onion in ¼ c. butter. Stir in mushrooms, crab, cracker crumbs, parsley, salt, and pepper. Spread mix over filets. Roll and place side down in baking dish.
3. In a sauce pan, melt 3 T. butter. Blend in flour and ¼ t. salt. Add enough milk to mushroom juice to make 1½ c.
4. Add wine in saucepan. Cook and stir until it thickens and bubbles. Pour over filets.
5. Bake at 400° for 25 minutes. Sprinkle with cheese and paprika. Return to oven and bake about 10 more minutes, or until fish flakes with a fork.

Serves 2-4.

STUFFED SPINACH

1½-2 c. spinach (fresh, raw)
3 tofu cakes
12-16 oz. raw cottage cheese (if available)
1 T. (heaping) dulse flakes (seaweed)
1 c. cooked brown rice
¼ c. sunflower seeds
1 large stalk celery, finely chopped
2 tsp. Jensen's seasoning or ½ t. VegeSal
Juice of 1 lemon (squeezed in to taste)

1. Wash spinach (preferably a slightly wilted bunch). While still damp, stuff individual leaves with above mixture, and roll up.
2. Use large pot with water and steamer unit inserted. Start water boiling and place rolled and closed spinach in steamer unit. (May be closed with toothpicks.)
3. Steam until warm throughout.
4. Serve immediately.

Serves 4-6.

SUSAN'S FRITADA

8 c. (heaping) raw zucchini, grated or sliced thin
3 c. (heaping) mushrooms, sliced
1 can artichoke hearts (8½ oz.)
¼ c. olive oil
3 T. butter
1 c. Parmesan cheese, grated
6 eggs
2 t. oregano
¼ t. salt
½ t. pepper
3 medium cloves of garlic

1. On a high flame, sauté half of the zucchini in ⅛ c. olive oil and 1 T. butter in an 8"-frying pan until translucent. Repeat with other half of zucchini, oil, and butter.
2. Place in oval or rectangular casserole dish (flat and low).
3. Pre-heat oven to 350°.
4. Sauté mushrooms on medium-high flame in 1 T. butter until brown. Add to casserole.
5. Drain canned artichoke hearts, quarter, and add to casserole dish.
6. In blender, mix together 6 eggs, Parmesan cheese, pepper, salt, and oregano. Pour over casserole.
7. Squeeze garlic through press over casserole. Bake approximately 25-30 minutes, until knife placed in center comes out dry.
8. Cut into squares.

Serves 4-6.

Serve hot or cold.

SWEET & SOUR TOFU WITH VEGETABLES

2 t. cornstarch
⅔ c. pineapple chunks with juice
1 T. apple cider vinegar
½ T. molasses
2 T. tamari
½ t. ginger (fresh)
2 T. oil
1 c. mung sprouts, chopped
½ c. water chestnuts, sliced
1 medium onion, chopped
1 large carrot, sliced diagonally
1 green pepper, chopped
¾ lb. tofu, cut into chunks
½ can kidney beans, drained
2 T. water

1. Dissolve cornstarch in 2 T. water, add ¼ c. pineapple juice, ¼ c. water, vinegar, molasses, tamari, and ginger. Set aside.
2. Heat oil in wok or large frying pan. Add onion and carrot, and cook a few minutes.
3. Add green pepper, sprouts, water chestnuts, beans, and tofu. Cover and cook over medium heat a few minutes.
4. Add remaining pineapple juice and chunks. Uncover and cook about 10 minutes.

Serves 4.

A good wok dish.

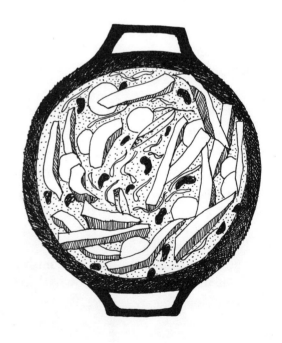

SWEET & SOUR CHICKEN

2 pkgs. chicken parts
3 large cans tomato paste
1 pt. pineapple juice
1 c. pitted prunes
2 green peppers, chopped
½ pineapple, chopped
1 T. honey
½ t. cinnamon
¼ t. nutmeg
1 t. salt
½ c. coconut, shredded
2T. molasses

1. Pre-heat oven to 375°.
2. Place chicken pieces in baking pan.
3. Mix together tomato paste and pineapple juice (about 2 parts tomato paste to 1 part juice).
4. Add honey, cinnamon, nutmeg, and salt.
5. Chop up green pepper and pineapple.
6. Pour sauce over chicken, add green pepper and pineapple, and cover with sesame seeds, prunes, and shredded coconut.
7. Bake approximately 1 hour or until chicken is tender.

TOFU ENCHILADA

Filling:

2 tofu cakes
2 6-oz. pkgs. soybean spread (may substitute 12 oz. ground cooked soybeans)
1 large carrot, grated
2 avocados
½ c. crushed almonds
1 t. Jensen's seasoning or ½ t. VegeSal
1 c. buckwheat groats, cooked
Herb salt

A good quick sauce:

1 can tomato bisque soup
½ c. milk
Hot sauce to taste
Grated cheese

1. Pre-heat oven to 400°.
2. Combine above mixture.
3. Roll up into a whole wheat tortilla that has been coated with oil and garlic salt.
4. Tuck ends in, cover with sauce, and bake at 400° for 10 minutes.

Yields 8-9 enchiladas.

TOFU TOSTADA

Oil or butter
Tortillas
Lettuce
Tomato
Carrots
Scallions
Cheese
Guacamole
Sour cream
Hot sauce
Tofu
Soy sauce
Garlic
Salt

1. Sauté in oil or butter one corn tortilla per serving. Be sure to pat off excess oil after cooking.
2. Line up on a tray, platter, or in bowls shredded lettuce, chopped tomatoes, chopped carrots, diced scallions, grated cheese, homemade guacamole, sour cream, and hot sauce.
3. Now mash up tofu into a buttered frying pan (1 carton tofu serves 4) and sauté about 5-7 minutes, until warm. Add tamari or soy sauce, ¼ c. per carton and 1 t. garlic granules per carton. Cook over low heat 5 minutes.
4. Top tortilla with tofu mixture, then cover with scoop of guacamole and handful of grated cheese. Cover with lettuce, tomato, carrots, scallions, hot sauce, and scoops of guacamole and sour cream.

A meal in itself — and a good introduction to tofu.

TUNA & WHEAT GERM QUICHE

12-oz. can of tuna, packed in water, well-drained
1 c. cheese, grated (half Jack, half Cheddar is excellent)
1 onion, chopped
2 stalks celery, chopped
½ c. zucchini or broccoli, drained well
1 c. evaporated skim milk
2 eggs
1 T. lemon juice
½ t. salt
1 t. basil
½ t. nutmeg

Crust:

1¼ c. melted butter
⅔ c. whole wheat flour
¼ c. wheat germ
2-4 t. water
½ of 1 egg white

1. Pre-heat oven to 450°.
2. Cut butter into flour for crust.
3. Stir in wheat germ, water, and egg white, and mix well.
4. Pat into a 9″-pie pan and bake for 10 minutes.
5. Sauté vegetables.
6. After crust is baked, pour tuna, sautéed vegetables, and cheese into crust.
7. Blend egg, milk, lemon juice, and seasonings, and pour over casserole.
8. Bake for 15 minutes. Reduce heat to 350° and continue baking for 12-15 minutes.

Serves 4-6.

VEGETABLE-CHEESE SOUFFLE

1 c. milk
2 c. broccoli, chopped
1 c. carrots, grated
1 c. mushrooms, sliced
¼ c. powdered milk
3 T. flour (unbleached)
1½ t. sea salt
⅛ t. pepper
½ t. cream of tartar
¼ t. basil
5 eggs
1½ c. Cheddar cheese, shredded
2-3 T. parsley, chopped
Butter

1. Pre-heat oven to 300°.
2. Heat 1 c. milk to simmer.
3. Blend powdered milk, unbleached white flour, salt, pepper, and basil.
4. Add to hot milk and cook over medium heat, stirring with wisk until sauce thickens.

5. Remove from heat and cool a bit. Add 4 egg yolks, shredded Cheddar cheese, and chopped parsley.
6. Add vegetables.
7. Beat 5 egg whites until stiff. Add salt, cream of tartar, and fold into sauce.
8. Pour into well-buttered deep casserole dish. Bake at 300° for 1 hour.

VEGETABLE PANCAKES

2 eggs, lightly beaten
½ c. cottage cheese
2 T. whole wheat flour
¼ c. wheat germ
1 t. butter
1 t. sea salt
¼ small onion, chopped
½ small zucchini, grated
1 carrot, grated

1. Thoroughly mix eggs, cottage cheese, flour, wheat germ, and butter to make a batter.
2. In butter, sauté onion, zucchini, and carrot. Drain.
3. Combine in batter.
4. Fry on hot oiled grill. Brown one side, turn and brown other side.

Serve with butter and soy sauce or tamari.

DESSERTS AND MUNCHIES

APPLE-OF-MY-EYE PIE

Crust:

2 c. whole wheat flour
1 t. salt
⅔ c. butter
5 T. cold water

Filling:

6 c. Pippin apples, thinly sliced
2 t. lemon juice
¾ c. brown sugar
½ t. nutmeg
½ t. cinnamon

1. Combine flour and salt. Cut in butter.
2. Sprinkle in water, one tablespoon at a time.
3. Form dough. Split into halves.
4. Roll out one half and lay into greased 9″-pie pan. Roll out other half and set aside.
5. Wash, peel, core, and thinly slice apples. Toss with lemon juice, and add sugar and spices. Mix well.
6. Pour mixture into pie pan, and cover with remaining dough. Pinch edges.
7. Bake at 425° for 30 minutes, with foil placed on top, but not sealed. Remove foil and bake 10-20 minutes longer.

Serves 6-8.

An all-American favorite.

CAROB-BANANA CHEESECAKE

Crust:

2 pkgs. wafers or graham crackers
1½ sticks butter, melted
1 T. honey

Filling:

1 lb. cream cheese (2 8-oz. pkg.)
2 eggs
½-⅔ c. honey
1 t. vanilla
2-3 T. (heaping) carob powder

Topping:

1 small carton sour cream
1 small ripe banana
1 t. vanilla

1. Pre-heat oven to 375°.
2. Mix crust ingredients and press into pyrex pie pan. Bake for 5-7 minutes in pre-heated oven.
3. In blender, cream together filling ingredients.
4. Pour into shell and bake at 375° for 30 minutes. Raise oven temperature to 425°.
5. Blend topping ingredients together. Spread topping over cake and bake at 425° for 5 minutes.
6. Chill.

Serves 4-6.

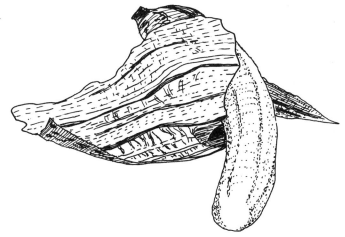

CAROB CRUNCH COOKIES

1 stick butter
¾ c. honey
2 t. vanilla
1 c. whole wheat flour or pastry flour, sifted
¾ t. baking soda
3 T. carob
1 T. peanut butter
½ c. sunflower seeds
Sprinkle salt

1. Pre-heat oven to 375°.
2. Cream butter, honey, and vanilla together.
3. Mix all ingredients together, and form into small round balls.
4. Bake on cookie sheet approximately 10 minutes.

Yields 1-2 dozen.

CAROB MOUSSE (Instant Carob Pudding)

2 c. Ricotta cheese
½ c. milk
2 t. vanilla
½ t. cinnamon
2 T. (level) carob powder
2 T. honey

1. Blend all ingredients in blender.
2. Chill.

Serves 4.

A quick gourmet dessert. Delicious topped with whipped cream, banana, or nuts.

CARROT COCONUT CAKE
(With Honey Cream Frosting)

½ c. melted butter or oil
2 eggs
¾-1 c. honey
2 c. carrots, grated
2 t. vanilla
2 c. whole wheat flour
2 t. cinnamon
½ t. nutmeg
¼ t. cloves
1 t. salt
1 T. baking powder
¼ c. soy grits
½ c. sunflower seeds or nuts
½-1 c. raisins
½ c. coconut, shredded

1. Pre-heat oven to 325°.
2. Mix first 5 ingredients together.
3. In a separate bowl, mix rest of ingredients together.
4. Mix all ingredients until smooth.
5. Pour into greased bread pans (1 small and 1 large, or 3 small).
6. Bake for 1 hour.

Serves 10-12.

HONEY CREAM FROSTING

Honey
Ricotta cheese
Cream cheese
Milk
Cinnamon
Coconut

Blend until desired consistency and frost.

CHRISTMAS COCONUT CAKE

1 c. unbleached white flour
1 c. whole wheat flour
½ t. salt
2 t. baking powder
½ c. raisins
½ c. coconut, shredded
½ c. melted butter
¾ c. honey
2 eggs
2-3 mashed bananas
1 t. vanilla
3 T. yogurt or buttermilk
Nuts or sunflower seeds (optional)

1. Pre-heat oven to 325°.
2. Oil one large loaf pan, or 3 small pans.
3. Combine flour, salt, baking powder, raisins, and coconut. Mix well.
4. In separate bowl, mix the butter, honey, eggs, bananas, vanilla, and buttermilk.
5. Combine all ingredients and pour into baking pan.
6. Bake 1½ hours.

Serves 6-8.

COCONUT COOKIES

1 c. honey
1 c. butter, melted
2 eggs
¾ c. yogurt or sour cream
1 t. salt
1½ t. baking powder
½ c. coconut, shredded
¾ c. raisins
1½ c. whole wheat pastry flour
½ c. soy flour

1. Pre-heat oven to 350°.
2. Combine all ingredients and place rounded teaspoons of mixture on ungreased cookie sheet.
3. Bake 12 minutes.

Yields 2-3 dozen.

COCONUT LEMON BREAD PUDDING

¼-½ c. honey
2 T. water
2 c. raw milk
1 T. lemon peel, grated
1 t. vanilla
6-7 slices egg bread or soft whole wheat bread (raisin bread tastes great, too)
2 T. butter
4 eggs
½ c. coconut, grated

1. Pre-heat oven to 375°.
2. Beat eggs.
3. Combine milk (preferably scalded), eggs, honey, vanilla, rind, water, butter, coconut, and bread.
4. Pour into buttered 1½ qt. baking dish.
5. Fill a pan with hot water and place baking dish inside. Place in oven, and bake 35-40 minutes until firm.

Serves 5-7.

Good for the Holidays.

CURRIED FRUIT EMILY

1 c. pineapple chunks
3 c. assorted fruit (peaches, apricots, apples, and pears), fresh, dried, mixed
¼ c. raisins and cashews
2 bananas, sliced and put in last to avoid discoloring
½ c. butter
2 t. curry
¼ c. brown sugar
2 t. honey
Dash olive oil
Dash fresh ginger, grated

1. Pre-heat oven to 275°.
2. Place fruit in casserole dish.
3. In separate frying pan, melt on very low flame ¼-½ c. butter. Add dash of olive oil. When melted, add 2 t. curry powder and the dash of ginger. Add fruit.
4. When mixture has stewed, add sugar and honey, and bake uncovered at 275° for 1 hour in casserole dish.
5. Add bananas and serve warm. The longer the curry is simmered in the butter, the more flavor is released, but be careful not to burn the butter.

Serves 4-6.

DIANE'S LEMON CHEESECAKE

Crust:

½ c. granola
½ c. walnuts, chopped
½ c. brown sugar or honey
2 t. cinnamon
½ c. butter, melted

Filling:

5 eggs
⅛ t. salt
1½ t. lemon juice
1½ t. lemon rind
2 pkg. 8-oz. soft cream cheese
3 T. whole wheat flour

1. Pre-heat oven to 350°.
2. Combine all crust ingredients and press into spring-form pan.
3. Combine all filling ingredients in blender or mixer bowl, and pour into crust.
4. Bake 1 hour.

Serves 6-8.

EASY, QUICK DESSERT

Strawberries
Sour cream
Brown sugar

1. Wash and stem fresh strawberries.
2. Place two bowls out, one filled with sour cream, the other with brown sugar.
3. Dip strawberries first in sour cream, then in brown sugar.
4. Place in mouth!

Great for the munchies.

FRUIT PUDDING

8 oz. Ricotta cheese
4 oz. cream cheese
1 c. peach or blueberry-flavored kefir
   (liquid yogurt)
2 ripe bananas
2 t. honey
1 small box strawberries
1 t. cinnamon
1 cantaloupe
½ c. raisins

1. Blend Ricotta cheese, cream cheese, kefir, 1 banana, honey, 6 strawberries, and cinnamon.
2. Cut cantaloupe in half and remove seeds.
3. Stuff mixture into cantaloupe half. Cover with raisins, strawberries, and banana slices.
4. Serve and enjoy.

Serves 2-4.

GERMAN CAROB CAKE

Cake:

1½ c. carob cookie crumbs
½ c. almonds, chopped
1½ T. brown sugar, or ¾ T. honey
¼ c. butter, melted
1 c. melted carob chips
3 pkgs. cream cheese (8 oz.), softened and
   whipped
⅔ c. honey
2 T. carob powder
5 eggs
1 t. vanilla
1 T. almond flavoring
3 T. whole wheat flour

Frosting:

5 T. brown sugar
5 T. butter
5 T. half & half
¾ c. coconut, shredded
¾ c. almonds, chopped

1. Combine first 4 cake ingredients and press into spring-form pan. Chill.
2. Combine carob chips, softened and whipped cream cheese, honey, carob powder, and 5 eggs, added one at a time.
3. Next add vanilla, almond flavoring, and whole wheat flour.
4. Pour into pan and bake at 350° for 45 minutes. Cool and refrigerate, preferably overnight.
5. Combine all frosting ingredients, except almonds, in saucepan. Boil approximately 3 minutes.
6. Cool, frost cake, and top with almonds.

Serves 8-10.

GODDESS DELIGHT FRUIT SUPREME

Salad:

Strawberries
Bananas
Pineapple
Apples
Pears
Peaches
Coconut
Currants
Nuts

Dressing:

5″×4″ wedge of watermelon without seeds
    (about 1½ c. juice)
4 dates
¼ c. pineapple juice
Juice of ½ lemon
Honey, to taste

1. Chop up salad ingredients.
2. Mix dressing in blender and cover fruit mixture.

The ultimate healthful indulgence.

HOMEMADE GRANOLA

4 c. rolled oats
½ c. sesame seeds
½ c. sunflower seeds
½ c. bran
½ c. almonds, cashews, or both
½ c. salt
¼ c. honey or maple syrup
¼ c. sesame oil
1 t. vanilla
½ c. raisins

1. Pre-heat oven to 350°.
2. Lightly heat honey, oil, and vanilla. Mix in dry ingredients and spread in shallow pan.
3. Bake for 40 minutes, stirring every 10 minutes.
4. Remove from oven and add raisins. It becomes crunchier when it cools.

Serves 8-10.

Optional suggestions: Add wheat germ, coconut, soy grits, dried fruit, cinnamon, dried apples, or powdered carob.

HONEY DATE CHEESECAKE
(From the Cheesecake Experience)

Filling:

2 8-oz. pkg. cream cheese
2 eggs
½ t. lemon juice
⅔ c. honey
6 dates (Medjol or barhi are best), pitted
1 t. vanilla extract

Topping:

1 c. sour cream
¾ t. vanilla extract
1½ t. honey

1. Pre-heat oven to 375°.
2. Cake may be made with a crust or without. Combine all filling ingredients into a blender or food processor. Blend until smooth.
3. Pour into pie dish or baking dish (over crust if you use one).
4. Bake at 375° for about 30 minutes. Do not overbake; the texture should be custard-like and still a little loose.
5. Take out of oven and cover with mixed topping.

(continued next column)

6. Place back in oven for 5-7 minutes.
7. Cool, chill, then serve.

Serves 6-8.

Creamy and rich.

HOT OR COLD BANANA CRÊPE

Use a crêpe, whole wheat chapati, or tortilla
1½ bananas per crêpe
½ t. honey per crêpe
Lemon juice
Currants and coconut
Sprinkle of cinnamon

1. Combine bananas, lemon juice, honey, currants, and coconut.
2. Take chapati and sprinkle with cinnamon.
3. Place banana mixture in layers, alternating with chapati, and cover with coconut. Bake in 350°-oven until warm.
4. Serve hot, or let sit in refrigerator overnight and eat cold.

JUDY'S CARROT CAKE

Cake:

1⅓ c. honey
1½ c. sesame oil
2 c. whole wheat flour
2 t. baking soda
3 t. cinnamon
4 eggs, slightly beaten
1½ c. walnuts, chopped
2½ c. raw carrots, grated
1 can crushed (or fresh) pineapple (8 oz.)
1 t. vanilla

Icing:

8 oz. cream cheese, softened
2-3 c. confectioner's sugar or brown sugar,
    or 1½ c. honey
Juice of 1-2 fresh oranges

1. Pre-heat oven to 350°.
2. Blend all ingredients together and place
   in 13″×9″×2″ greased casserole dish.
3. Bake at 350° for 45-50 minutes.
4. Top with icing, if desired.

Serves 12-15.

MICHAEL'S APPLE CRISP

3 c. rolled oats
2½ c. whole wheat pastry flour
1 T. baking soda
1 t. salt
1 c. honey
1 c. oil (sesame is good)
6-8 apples, washed, cored and thinly sliced
⅓ c. wheat germ
⅓ c. sunflower seeds
1 t. ginger
1 t. cinnamon
1 t. nutmeg
1 t. allspice

1. Pre-heat oven to 350°.
2. In a bowl, combine all ingredients except apples. Mix or work through with
   hands.
3. Sprinkle mixture over apple slices in a
   baking dish. Bake 30-40 minutes until
   brown.

Serves 5-7.

Great served warm with honey ice cream.

NO-BAKE CREAMY PEACH PIE

3 small cartons peach yogurt
1 c. whipped cream
4-5 T. Drambuie (may substitute orange juice or 1 t. extract)
1 t. vanilla
1 pkg. honey-sweetened cookies (or brown sugar), wafer style
1 c. melted butter
2 T. brown sugar or honey
2 bananas
2 sliced peaches
Cinnamon
Almonds

1. Crush the wafers by hand or in food processor. Add sugar or honey, and pour melted butter slowly into mixture until desired consistency (not oily).
2. Add cinnamon and press into large pie pan.
3. Mix yogurt, whipped cream, Drambuie and vanilla, and pour into pie shell. Top with almonds, sliced bananas and peaches.
4. Refrigerate and serve chilled.

Serves 6-8.

NO-DAIRY BANANA ICE CREAM

Bananas, frozen
Whatever you want to add

1. Peel bananas and place in freezer until frozen.
2. Put through juicer, or blender, and add frozen strawberries, peaches, etc.
3. If desired, carob powder or honey may be added.
4. Top with nuts and coconut.

This is a delicious treat with no dairy products or sweeteners. Good for raw food eaters, and for those allergic to milk.

NO SWEETENER DESSERT

Yogurt
Cottage cheese
Cinnamon
Your favorite fruit

1. Mix together equal parts yogurt and cottage cheese.
2. Add cinnamon and your favorite fruit.

PEACH COBBLER

1 c. peaches, sliced
⅛ c. honey
¼ t. almond extract
1 t. sesame seeds
⅓ c. wheat germ
½ t. cinnamon
1½ t. whole wheat flour
1 t. water
¼ t. baking powder
1 t. butter

1. Pre-heat oven to 425°.
2. Mix all ingredients.
3. Put into small baking tins.
4. Bake at 425° until hot and bubbling (about 10-15 minutes)
5. Serve hot with ice cream, or cold.

Serves 3-4.

Ummmm.

PERSIMMON PUDDING

1 c. persimmon purée (2-3 persimmons,
   depending upon size, peeled, and
   mashed in blender)
2 t. baking soda
1 c. date sugar (or half sugar, half honey)
½ t. cinnamon
½ t. nutmeg
1 egg, well beaten
1 t. vanilla
1 c. milk
½ t. salt
2 T. butter
1 c. whole wheat flour
¼ c. raisins
½ c. dates or currants
½ c. nuts, chopped

1. Place persimmon purée, sugar (honey),
   egg, milk, butter, and vanilla in blender, and blend until smooth.
2. Sift all dry ingredients together, except
   nuts.
3. Mix the wet with the dry, and add
   dates, raisins, and nuts.
4. Pour into greased coffee can or baking
   dish (round with hole in center comes
   out nicest). Set in shallow pan of hot
   water.
5. Bake at 325° for 1½ hours. Be sure to
   grease the mold or pan with butter or
   margarine, rather than oil.
6. When done, remove from water, let
   cool a bit, and invert on platter.

*With hole in the center, fill with a mound of
yogurt or vanilla ice cream, if desired.*

PETER'S SIERRA NEVADA PUMPKIN CAKE

1 large can pumpkin
1 c. butter
½ c. brown sugar
½ c. honey
2 eggs
1 c. coconut, shredded
½ c. sunflower seeds
1 T. cinnamon
½ t. cloves, ground
1 T. baking powder
1 t. salt
2 c. whole wheat flour
1 c. unbleached white flour
½ c. raisins
½ c. water

Topping:

¾ lb. cream cheese
Brown sugar or whipped honey
Cinnamon
Squeeze of lemon

1. Pre-heat oven to 350°.
2. Mix all ingredients and place in 2 regular loaf pans (or 1 large and 2 small).
3. Bake 1½ hours.

Cool and frost.

PUMPKIN CHEESECAKE

Crust:

2 pkgs. honey or brown sugar sweetened
    wafers or graham crackers
3 T. honey
1½ sticks butter, melted

Filling:

1 lb. cream cheese (2 8-oz. pkgs.)
2 eggs
⅔ c. honey or 1 c. brown sugar
⅛ c. pumpkin, cooked (canned is fine)
1 t. cinnamon
1 t. vanilla
Sprinkle of salt

Topping:

1 large carton sour cream
⅓ c. honey
1 t. vanilla
2 t. cinnamon
3 T. pumpkin

1. Pre-heat oven to 375°.
2. Crush graham crackers or wafers. (A food processor is great!) Mix with melted butter and honey, and press into large pyrex baking dish.
3. Combine all filling ingredients with hand mixer or blender on low speed, and pour into crust. Bake about 30 minutes (until custard-like when shaken).
4. Remove and raise oven temperature to 425°.
5. Combine topping ingredients and pour over filling. Bake at 425° for 5 minutes.

Serves 6-8.

Good for the Holidays — popular anytime. It never fails to please.

MANDARIN CHOCOLATE CHEESECAKE

*Use exactly the same recipe as above, except substitute 2 T. cocoa for pumpkin, and ¾ t. orange extract and ¼ t. almond extract for vanilla in filling. For topping use 1 t. cocoa and no cinnamon or pumpkin.

RAW BANANA CREAM PIE

1 medium-sized bunch bananas
1 carton raw cream
1½ c. cashews or almonds, crushed or ground
1 c. currants (20 or so dates or figs)
2 T. nut butter
Sesame oil

1. Combine almonds, dash of oil, nut butter, and either dates, currants, raisins, or figs.
2. Line pyrex pie dish with crust.
3. Crush and cream the ripe bananas, place in crust, and cover with whipped cream, coconut, sliced almonds.
4. Refrigerate and serve chilled.

Serves 6-8.

RAW MOCHA PUDDING

16 oz. Ricotta cheese
⅔ c. milk
3 T. honey
1 t. vanilla
1 t. cinnamon
1 t. instant coffee
4 T. carob

1. Combine all ingredients in a blender.
2. Blend until creamy.
3. Chill and eat.

RICE PUDDING

1 c. milk
2 eggs
1½ T. honey
⅛ t. vanilla
⅛ t. lemon juice
1 c. cooked rice
¼ c. raisins
½ t. cinnamon

1. Pre-heat oven to 325°.
2. Mix all ingredients and pour into small baking tins.
3. Bake at 325° for 35-45 minutes.

Serves 3-4.

RICOTTA PLUM PUDDING

1 large carton Ricotta cheese
¾ c. raw milk
3 T. plum jam
½ c. currants
1 t. vanilla
½ t. cinnamon (or 1 T. coconut, optional)

1. Place all ingredients in blender for quick mix.
2. Pour into custard dishes and top with currants and cinnamon (or coconut).
3. Refrigerate and serve chilled.

Serves 4.

RONA'S LOW CALORIE ALMOND CHEESECAKE

4 large eggs
2 c. cottage cheese
1 c. sour cream
⅓ c. honey
6 T. whole wheat flour
2 t. almond extract
1½ t. vanilla
½ c. almonds, sliced

1. Pre-heat oven to 350°.
2. Place 2 eggs in blender with half the cottage cheese, sour cream, flour, vanilla, and almond extract. Blend and pour mixture into bowl. Repeat with remaining eggs, etc.
3. In bowl, add honey and beat well.
4. Pour into lightly greased pan and bake for about 1 hour. Oven may need to be turned down to 300°. It is done when cheesecake does not cling to toothpick.
5. Cook, chill, and serve.

Serves 6-8.

RUTH'S RAW CANDIES

½ c. honey
½ c. tahini
½ c. dry milk
½ c. coconut, shredded
½ c. sunflower seeds
½ c. raisins, chopped

1. Heat honey and tahini over low flame.
2. Mix separately the dry milk, coconut, seeds, and raisins.
3. Blend all ingredients and form into balls.
4. Chill and serve.

STUFFED DATES

Dates
Tahini
Coconut
Walnuts
Orange juice

1. Pit dates.
2. Fill with mixture of tahini, coconut, walnuts, and a splash of orange juice.

TERRI'S CHEESECAKE COOKIE SQUARES

1 c. whole wheat flour
⅓ c. butter, softened
⅔ c. brown sugar
½ c. walnuts, chopped
1 pkg. cream cheese (8 oz.)
1 egg
2 T. milk
2 T. lemon juice
½ t. vanilla

1. Pre-heat oven to 350°.
2. Combine flour, butter, ⅓ c. brown sugar, and blend with mixer until fine. Add walnuts.
3. Reserving 1 c. of mixture for topping, press remainder into ungreased, 8"-square pan. Bake for 12-15 minutes, until lightly browned.
4. In same bowl, combine remaining ingredients. Blend well and spread over crust. Make sure this includes the reserved 1 c. of crumb mixture above.
5. Bake at 350° for 25-30 minutes. Cool and cut into squares.

Serves 9-12.

ZUCCHINI NUT CAKE

3 eggs, well beaten
1 c. oil
3 c. flour
2 c. brown sugar
2 c. zucchini, grated
1 c. walnuts, chopped
1 t. each baking soda, baking powder, salt,
    and cinnamon
2 t. vanilla

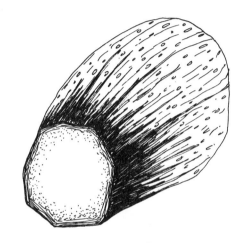

1. Pre-heat oven to 325°.
2. Mix together all ingredients and pour
   into bundt cake pan.
3. Bake 1¼ hours. Makes 1 large cake.

Serves 6-8.

*If desired, put a glaze on after cake is cool by
mixing 1 T. milk with 1 c. of sifted, powdered
sugar.*

SMOOTHIES, ETC.

APPLE-BANANA ENERGY SMOOTHIE

6 oz. fresh apple juice
2 oz. milk
1 banana
1 T. Brewer's yeast
½ t. bee pollen (optional)

Blend.

Serves 1.

Good in the morning.

AVOCADO CARROT MILKSHAKE

1 c. fresh carrot juice
½ avocado

1. Place ingredients in blender, and blend at medium speed.
2. If too thick or thin, adjust ingredients accordingly.
3. Drink immediately.

Serves 1.

This makes a great pick-me-up or quick lunch. Don't let the sound of it disturb you — it tastes delicious!

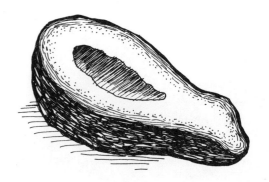

BARB & LARRY'S FAVORITE SMOOTHIE

2 c. apple juice
1 banana
8-10 frozen strawberries
2 T. protein powder
2-3 T. yogurt
1 egg

Blend.

Serves 2.

CAROB SMOOTHIE

2 oz. apple juice
4 oz. milk
1 scoop vanilla honey ice cream
1 T. (heaping) carob powder
1 egg
Dash cinnamon

Blend.

Serves 1.

CITRUS COOLER

4 oz. orange juice
2 oz. pineapple juice
1 scoop lime sherbert

Blend.

Serves 1.

PAPAYA SMOOTHIE

½ fresh papaya
4 oz. milk
2 T. plain yogurt
2 T. lemon juice
1 t. honey

Blend.

Serves 1.

COCONUT MILKSHAKE

2 oz. coconut milk
4 oz. milk
1 scoop vanilla honey ice cream
1 T. shredded coconut.

Blend and serve topped with a slice of pineapple.

Serves 1.

SUNRISE SPECIAL

6 oz. orange juice, fresh squeezed
1 egg
2 T. (heaping) plain yogurt
1½ frozen bananas

Put in blender and blend until smooth.

Serves 1.

Great breakfast drink.

INDEX

Other Books from
Whatever Publishing, Inc.

At Your Age You're Having A What?! by Rita Abrams, illustrated by
   Ellen Blonder
Being Beautiful by Zia Wesley-Hosford
Creative Visualization by Shakti Gawain
Creative Visualization Workbook by Shakti Gawain
How to Manage Your Boss by Christopher Hegarty
Tantra for the West — *A Guide to Personal Freedom* by Marcus Allen
Reunion: Tools for Transformation by Marcus Allen and Shakti
   Gawain (with Jon Bernoff)
14 Days to a Wellness Lifestyle by Dr. Donald Ardell
Prospering Woman by Ruth Ross
The Dolphins' Gift by Elizabeth Gawain
Astrology for the New Age — *An Intuitive Approach* by Marcus
   Allen
Chrysalis — *A Journey into the New Spiritual America* by Marcus
   Allen
Seeds to the Wind — Poems, Songs, Meditations by Marcus Allen

Write for a free catalog of fine books, records, and tapes from:

Whatever Publishing, Inc.
P.O. Box 137, Mill Valley, CA 94941

Phone: (415) 388-2100

Order toll free (800) 227-3900
In California (800) 632-2122